The
Victorious Christ

The Victorious Christ

A STUDY OF THE BOOK OF REVELATION

C. FREEMAN SLEEPER

Westminster John Knox Press
Louisville, Kentucky

© 1996 C. Freeman Sleeper

Book design by Jennifer K. Cox
Cover design by Alec Bartsch
Cover illustration: Ascension from the Mount of Olives, *James J. Tissot, 1836–1902. French. Courtesy of SuperStock.*

First edition

Published by Westminster John Knox Press
Louisville, Kentucky

This book is printed on acid-free paper that meets the American National Standards Institute Z39.48 standard. ∞

PRINTED IN THE UNITED STATES OF AMERICA

96 97 98 99 00 01 02 03 04 05 — 10 9 8 7 6 5 4 3 2 1

Library of Congress Cataloging-in-Publication Data
Sleeper, C. Freeman (Charles Freeman)
    The victorious Christ : a study of the book of Revelation / C. Freeman Sleeper.
        p.   cm.
    Includes index.
    ISBN 0-664-25620-1 (alk. paper)
    1. Bible. N.T. Revelation—Criticism, interpretation, etc.
I. Title.
BS2825.2.S64   1996
228'.06—dc20
                                            96-18499

This book is dedicated to those Pauls
who have helped me
to understand and appreciate scripture:

PAUL THE APOSTLE
PAUL MEYER
PAUL MINEAR
PAUL SCHUBERT

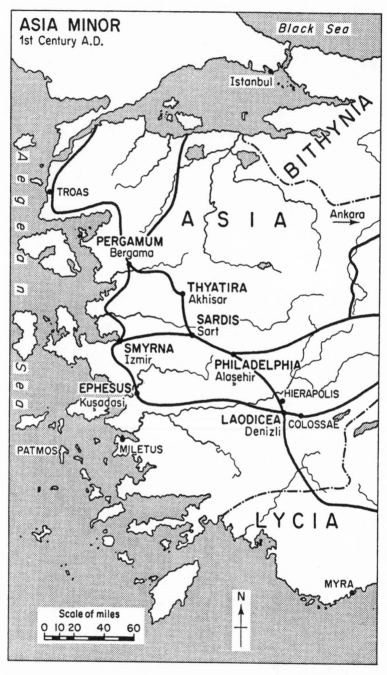

The setting for Revelation. (From J.P.M. Sweet, *Revelation*, Westminster Pelican Commentary, p. xvi. Philadelphia: Westminster Press, 1979.)

CONTENTS

PREFACE

On January 1, 1995, the *Washington Post* magazine section featured an article by Peter Carlson on "The Vision Thing." In it he surveyed some of the growing speculation about the year 1999 and the turn of the millennium. He quotes Hillel Schwartz there as saying, "Like it or not, there has always been something woo-woo about the year 2000." A major source of that speculation, of course, has been the book of Revelation.

When I first taught courses in New Testament, I used to avoid Revelation because I thought my students would not be able to understand it, even with my help. In recent years, I have found myself more and more interested in Revelation because of its sophisticated use of symbols and images. These are not the reflections of a junkie who had a good drug trip; nor are they the confused musings of a hack writer. As my appreciation has grown, so has that of students in my undergraduate courses and adult classes. That does not mean all the mysteries have been solved.

However, in working with John's text, I began to realize that many commentaries get in the way of the text, at least for a nonspecialist. They often begin with an introduction that answers all the historical and literary questions before one has a chance to ask them. Or they may sketch out a theological scheme that one is supposed to apply in reading the text. Also, most commentaries proceed verse by verse from the beginning, so that one doesn't really get a feel for the whole book until the end.

For that reason, we will begin in part 1 by reading the text as we would a modern novel or a mystery story. We will simply ask the basic questions anyone must ask in order to understand any story. In part 2, we will focus on images of conflict and violence in Revelation; then in part 3, we will look at some of those same images in other biblical and extrabiblical texts. Only in part 4 will we deal with the more difficult issues of interpretation and spell out some implications of Revelation for Christian living today.

In a "Family Circus" comic strip that appeared in 1992, Jeffy is telling his sister: "I'll tell you the difference between TV, radio, and books. *TV* puts stuff into your mind with pictures and sound. You don't even hafta think. *Radio* puts stuff into your mind with just sounds and words. You make up your own pictures. *Books* are quiet friends. They let you make up your own pictures *and* sounds. They make you *think!*" We need to approach Revelation with that kind of attitude.

In 1986, I was fortunate enough to attend a summer seminar funded by the National Endowment for the Humanities (NEH). It was led by Dr. Howard Clark Kee, then at Boston University, and focused on the contributions of the social sciences to interpreting the New Testament. My serious study of Revelation really began that summer, so this book is the completion of a long project. In the summer of 1993, I attended another NEH Summer Seminar at Cornell University, led by Dr. Calum Carmichael on the topic of law and religion in the Bible. Most of my research that summer was on the image of God as warrior in the Hebrew Bible, along with the relevance of this image to Revelation. I am indebted to both those mentors and especially to the National Endowment for the Humanities, without whose help this book would not have been possible.

Also helpful have been the sessions I attended of the Society of Biblical Literature seminar, "Reading the Apocalypse: The Intersection of Literary and Social Methods," where I always felt welcomed as a visitor.

Much of the material in this book was tested in classes at Roanoke College in Salem, Virginia. David Hudson, a religion and philosophy major, did a lot of filing for me. In 1995, I took early retirement from Roanoke after nineteen years there in order to write this and other books.

I am especially indebted to the faculty and staff of Union Theological Seminary in Virginia, where I am spending the 1995–96 academic year as a research fellow. Without access to its library and other facilities, this book could not have been completed on time.

The first draft of this manuscript was completed before I was able to see a book that I have included in the bibliography by Pablo Richard, the Latin American biblical scholar. During February of 1996, I not only read his book but observed a class he was teaching at Union Seminary and was able to have several conversations with him. As a result of those meetings with him, if there had been more time for revisions, I am sure I would have said a number of things differently.

One of the participants in the summer seminar at Cornell was an accomplished pianist. Once he related a story about his piano teacher, who had stopped his playing to ask what he was doing. "Why, I'm trying to play with some expression," was his reply. "Don't," warned his teacher. "Just play the notes."

Shortly after hearing that story, I heard a radio program of Bach's organ music, and the commentator said, "The Bach ideal is in the imagination—both his and ours."

These anecdotes represent two different ways of reading and listening. I invite you to use the second approach as you read the Revelation to John.

PART ONE

Looking at the Text

CHAPTER 1

Revelation
as a Multimedia Event

Today our world is dominated by a communications revolution. Nearly every day we may hear or read about a new or proposed development: an "information highway" or "cyberspace" or "interactive media" or "virtual reality." In contrast, earlier cultures tended to emphasize one or two means of communication: the spoken word (oral tradition); visual arts (pictorial representation, architecture); plays or musical drama; the printed word. What is new is the ability to combine several of these formats, to change them almost constantly, and to distribute them simultaneously to vast numbers of people.

The book we study here was, in its own time, an example of "virtual reality." It is much more than a "book," in the usual sense of a series of written words on a page. Through a variety of imaginative forms, the author tried to draw his audience into a different world. This other world was infinitely more real than the one they experienced every day, and it had the power to transform their lives.

If we are going to appreciate that author's message, we must prepare to encounter it for the first time. For some of you, it may in fact be the first time. If so, prepare for an adventure of the kind you had when you read about J.R.R. Tolkien's hobbit or C. S. Lewis's land of Narnia, or when you watched *E. T.* or *Star Wars*. On the other hand, if you think you already know how to solve all the puzzles and mysteries that the author of Revelation presents, you may still be in for a surprise. Put aside for now all your solutions, if you can. Transport yourself back in time nearly two thousand years. Try to hear the author's message with the same sense of wonder that those who had never heard it before felt.

WHAT KIND OF LITERATURE IS THIS?

EXERCISE 1

Fortunately the author did not want his audience to be completely mystified. He has provided an introduction and a conclusion to orient us. *Read* Revelation 1:1–11 and 22:6–21. Be prepared to discuss what you learn about the author and his book.

Who Wrote the Book?

We don't have to read very far to learn the name of the author. Three different times he identifies himself as John (1:1, 9; 22:8). Unfortunately he does not give us very much personal information. He says simply that he is a "servant" of Jesus Christ (1:1), a term that is also used in 22:6 and implied in 22:9. The Greek word that John used can be translated into English equally well as "slave" or "servant," so the idea is clearly that John has devoted himself to this master.

John does not claim for himself any of the titles that are used for other leaders of the early church, such as "apostle" or "deacon" or "elder" (*presbyteros*) or "bishop" (*episkopos*). The only other term he uses for himself is "brother." In Revelation 1:9, he claims to be a brother and fellow sufferer with his audience. In 22:9, the angel links him with other brothers who are early Christian prophets. The term "prophet," then, is one that is given to John, not one he explicitly claims for himself. As we shall see, he functions as other Christian prophets when he speaks a message that he has received from Jesus Christ, both directly (in visions) and indirectly (through angels). In other words, John does not claim any special authority over the churches to which he writes other than that of the message itself.

We do learn one other piece of information about John in 1:9. He is on the island of Patmos. His being there has something to do with the message that he calls "the word of God and the testimony of Jesus." (This is an echo of 1:2, which has the longer designation "of Jesus Christ.") The last phrase in both cases can mean the testimony that he has received *from* Jesus, or the message *about* him, or more likely a combination of both meanings. The implication is that John is not on the island voluntarily, but he gives us no other information to explain his presence. At this point, we are interested in looking at the book only as a piece of literature. Later (in part 4) we will see whether there is information from other sources that can tell us more about John as the author.

What Does John Say about His Book?

Again, we do not have to read very far to find the first answer to this question. In the opening verse, John calls his writing a "revelation" of (that is, *from*) Jesus Christ (1:1). Notice that the term is in the singular; the frequently heard plural "revelations" is simply not in the text. Even though the book is a composite of different kinds of material, from beginning to end it consists of *the* revelation to John. Since *apokalypsis* is the Greek word for "revelation," the book is often referred to as "the Apocalypse of John" or simply as "the Apocalypse."

This revelation is the disclosure of heavenly secrets, of "virtual reality." John's message is ultimately from God, but the reception process can involve a number of stages: from God to Jesus Christ through one or more angels (divine messengers) to John and other servants (1:1–2). John, in turn, shares it with the churches to which he is commanded to write (1:4, 11; also 22:16). The content of the message will emerge later, in reading other sections of John's book. In this opening section, he conveys a sense of urgency. The revelation describes events that are to happen soon (1:1); the time is near (1:3); Jesus Christ is coming with the clouds (1:7). The same point is made even more dramatically in the closing section, where the risen Christ says repeatedly, "I am coming soon" (22:7, 12, 20). The disclosure of divine secrets and the sense of urgency, then, are two characteristics of this literature, which John calls apocalyptic.

The revelation comes to John in a variety of ways. That is why I referred to it earlier as a multimedia document. It consists of what Jesus Christ showed him and others (1:1), so it includes "all that he [John] *saw*" (1:2). The book, then, contains a series of visions. At the same time, the revelation consists of what John *heard*: the word of God and the testimony of Jesus (1:2) and Christ's voice like a trumpet (1:10). The identity of the angel who speaks to John in 22:9 is not really clear, but in 22:12–13, 16, and 20 there is no doubt that it is Christ himself speaking. In 22:8, John twice claims authenticity for what he *heard and saw*. This language of seeing and hearing, of visions and auditions, continues throughout John's message.

What is astonishing is that John does not stop there. He *hears* Christ telling him to *"write in a book* what you *see"* (1:10–11). The text, then, is not a purely literary work in the sense in which we think of a novel or a short story. It can be understood only as a

literary record of what John heard and saw, as an introduction to
the world of symbols through which he tries to describe virtual
reality. Elisabeth Schüssler Fiorenza, one of the leading contemporary scholars on Revelation, captures this nicely by calling
John's book a "symphony of images."[1] In later chapters we will be
looking at those images, particularly images of conflict.

What else does John say about his book? When he refers to the
act of writing, he uses a second descriptive term. Not only is it a
book of revelation, it is a book of prophecy (1:3; 22:6–7, 10,
18–19). Just as Israel's prophets received the "word of God" and
interpreted it for events in their own time, so early Christian
prophets proclaimed and recorded messages that they received
from the risen Christ.[2] This is confirmed in a crucial passage in
19:10. As in the passage we have already examined in 22:9, an angel tells John not to worship him, since the angel and John are fellow servants. Then comes an explanation, apparently from John
himself: "For the testimony of Jesus is the spirit of prophecy."

We still have not exhausted what John tells us about his book.
It was meant to be read aloud, as were Paul's letters, probably in
the context of public worship. This is not surprising, since no duplicating equipment or overhead projectors were available then.
The general rate of literacy in the society of John's time was low,
and we can assume that it was not much higher among his audience. However, those who heard the book as it was being read
were warned to keep it (1:3; 22:18). For John, then, the process of
communication includes a moral dimension. A number of scholars have suggested that Revelation was actually meant to be per-
formed as a kind of religious drama. There is certainly some truth
to this insight, since there are appropriate places for the congregations to respond as they heard the book being read. But the context would almost certainly be that of worship and not a public
arena. Even though this performance-oriented view of Revelation
reinforces our understanding of it as a multimedia document, we
will not here pursue that view in more detail.[3]

WHO WAS JOHN'S AUDIENCE?

EXERCISE 2

You already know that John wrote to seven churches (1:11). If you
look at the map opposite the table of contents, you will see that

they are clustered in the western part of Asia Minor (modern Turkey). For more information about these churches, read Revelation 2—3.

What can we learn about John's audience from what he tells us? For now we will assume that we have no outside sources and that we must rely only on the information that John gives us.

We should note, however, that these letters do not claim to represent John's own words. He simply relays a message in which each letter follows a standard formula, as you have probably noticed. It is the risen Christ who speaks at the beginning of each letter ("These are the words of him who ... "). Christ is identified in each case by a symbol drawn from John's initial vision in 1:12–20. In a red-letter edition of the Bible, these words appear in red, even though they were not spoken by the man Jesus of Nazareth. For the early Christians, their Lord was alive and continued to speak to the churches through the mouth and pen of the prophets. Also, before each letter closes, another part of the formula identifies the words as what the Spirit is saying to the churches. John, then, is doing exactly what a Christian prophet was supposed to do. He is speaking as a Christ-filled or Spirit-filled messenger. He is a genuine charismatic figure.[4]

The first and most obvious point about John's audience is that he was writing to other Christians in those seven cities. In the opening section, as we saw, he had already identified with them in their deliverance (1:5–6) as well as in "the persecution and the kingdom and the patient endurance" (1:9, typical of John's style by putting things in sets of three). Even more obvious is the fact that each of the seven letters is addressed "to the church in ... " and draws to a close with this warning: "Let anyone who has an ear listen to what the Spirit is saying to the churches."

Second, it is also clear that these Christians were facing different kinds of conflict. Although we will examine this theme more thoroughly below in chapter 5, for now we can simply observe that in these churches the conflict was both internal and external. Internally, it involved false teachings or false practices within the congregations at Ephesus (2:2, 6), Pergamum (2:14–15), and Thyatira (2:20–23). In Thyatira, those who had listened to the false prophet Jezebel would face great "distress" unless they repented (2:22). Externally, there was the threat of serious harassment. Christians at Smyrna had already faced some kind of "affliction"

(2:9) and were facing worse trouble in the form of temporary imprisonment (2:10). The churches in Smyrna and Philadelphia were being harassed by the "synagogue of Satan" (2:9 and 3:9). Christians in Smyrna had to deal not only with Satan's throne but also with the fact that Antipas, apparently one of their members, had been killed (2:13).

A third observation is that the congregations were responding to these conflicts in different ways. You may have noticed that in these seven letters part of the formula is a pattern of praise and blame, good news and bad news. Another term that we saw in 1:9 is "patient endurance." It is used as a term of praise in the letters to Ephesus (2:2, 3), Thyatira (2:19), and Philadelphia (3:10). There is praise for those who resisted the false teachers in Ephesus (2:6) and Thyatira (2:24). There is also praise for those in Smyrna (2:9–10) and Pergamum (2:13) and Philadelphia (3:8) who remained steadfast and who did not deny their faith in the face of external threats. Blame, on the other hand, is directed at the Ephesians for having lost the enthusiasm of their first love (2:4), at Christians in Sardis for being dead or asleep (3:1–3), at the Laodiceans for being lukewarm (3:15–16), and especially at those Christians in Pergamum and Thyatira who tolerated false teachers (2:14–15 and 2:20). What standard was being used to determine praise or blame? Quite obviously, it was the extent to which the churches remained dedicated and faithful, even in the face of conflict.

A fourth point is that we do not learn very much about the socioeconomic situation of these churches. What a striking contrast the text makes between the Christians in Smyrna (2:9), who are poor (in economic terms) yet rich (in their faithfulness), and those in Laodicea who boasted about their wealth but deserved only to be pitied (3:17). Similarly, we learn that the church in Philadelphia had little power but remained committed even though a time of testing threatened it (3:8–10).

As we read more of Revelation, we will be able to add to our image of what John's original audience was like. However, today John's audience is no longer limited to the Christians in those seven cities of Asia Minor. Because his book was preserved and eventually made part of the church's collection of scripture, we have to recognize that we too are now part of the audience. Even though John did not have us in mind when he wrote what he heard and saw, the book is now addressed to us as well. We cannot help reading it from the perspective of our own time and place; but we can resist the temptation to try to force our ideas onto John's text, and instead listen to what the Spirit is saying today to the churches where we live.

QUESTIONS FOR DISCUSSION

1. Think of situations in which you have had multimedia or multisensory experiences. If you are in a group, share some of those experiences. Do you agree that John's message has some of the same qualities? Why do you agree or disagree?

2. In recent thinking, ministry involves three roles: pastoral, priestly, and prophetic. When John talks about his relationship to the churches, does he fit that model? Can you think of any church leader(s) today like John?

3. Based on what you have read so far, do you feel that a sense of urgency is central to John's message? If so, what do you think he meant by "soon"?

4. Do you believe that even though Christ had been crucified he continued to communicate through people like John? How would you know whether John was telling the truth?

5. If you were a member of one of the seven churches and you heard these letters read in your congregation, would you know exactly what you had to do? In other words, would you know what kind of behavior was expected of you?

CHAPTER 2

The Plot

Imagine that you are walking along a nature trail or through an enclosed tropical birdhouse at a major zoo or touring an exhibit at an art museum. One way to travel the route is to pause and read every sign, to try to observe every detail, to gain one piece of information at a time. Using this approach, you would accumulate a mass of details and eventually try to figure out how they fit into a larger pattern. A second approach is to walk the entire tour quickly. On your first trip you can get an overall impression of what to see and what is worth learning more about. You begin with a general impression of the whole tour or exhibit. Then you can go back again and again, each time noticing details that you missed before.

As noted in the preface, our way of reading Revelation is different from the usual pattern. Most commentaries take the first approach, looking at a few verses or a chapter at a time and then stopping to explain the meaning of words and phrases in that section. Instead, we will take the second approach, reading all the way through Revelation a number of times, each time looking for something new. By doing this, we can keep the general pattern of the book in mind, even while we examine particular features of John's earthscape and heavenscape.

Revelation does not have a "plot" in the sense of a narrative work such as a modern novel or a mystery story. As a dramatic work about coming events, however, it does have a structure. Hardly any two persons agree on all the details of that structure, but at this stage we can at least look for its main features.

JOHN AS MESSENGER

EXERCISE 3

In the introduction and the conclusion to his book, John has told us that he is recording what he has heard and seen. Now you are ready for your first trip through Revelation as a whole. As you read, ask yourself, "What *kinds* of things did John see?" Don't get bogged down in details, but look for blocks of material or sets of visions.

John as Observer

One of the things you probably discovered is that John is more of an onlooker than a participant. For the most part he is an observer, not an actor.

In 1:12–20, John reports that a heavenly figure appeared to him and commanded him to write this book. There are two obvious clues that the figure is the risen Christ. One is the phrase "one like the Son of Man" (1:13), a title used frequently by Jesus in the first three Gospels. The other is the claim that "I was dead, and see, I am alive forever and ever; and I have the keys of Death and of Hades" (1:18).

The next major vision, in chapters 4 and 5, involves a dramatic shift of location. John is taken up in the Spirit to heaven, where he sees God's throne, surrounded by various attendants, and a rather extraordinary Lamb. In the rest of the book, that Lamb becomes the dominant figure, as we shall see. In this first encounter, the Lamb is declared to be the only being capable of opening a scroll, which presumably contains some of the secrets that John is to reveal.

In chapters 6 and 7, John watches as the seven seals that enclose the scroll are broken, one by one. As this process is under way, John sees other groups that are part of the heavenly scene: the souls of those under the altar; 144,000 of Israel; and a great multitude from every nation.

Chapters 8 and 9 are much more of a multimedia event. John sees seven angels holding trumpets. As each trumpet is blown, John has an image of a different plague that will occur on earth. Before the seventh trumpet sounds (in 11:15–19), two other visions intervene. In chapter 10, an angel descends from heaven with a second scroll, which John proceeds to eat, signifying an additional message that he must deliver. The other is not exactly a vision. Rather, it is John's narrative description of what happens to the two witnesses (11:3) or prophets (11:10).

In chapters 12—13, John pictures a life-and-death struggle between a dragon (identified as the Devil and Satan) and a woman and her children, followed by two beasts who exercise the authority of the dragon. This is followed in chapter 14 by another vision of the 144,000, who are clearly identified as followers of the Lamb. Then three angels appear to announce the fact that Babylon is about to receive God's final judgment, pictured as a bloody harvest.

This announcement is followed in chapters 15—16 by a third set of seven plagues, symbolized this time not by seals or trumpets but by seven bowls. These bowls of wrath then provide the setting for the destruction of Babylon, which is described in vivid detail in chapters 17 and 18, followed in 19:1–10 by a great celebration in heaven.

From 19:11 through 22:5, John describes a complicated series of events, many of which are introduced with the phrase "Then I saw." These visions include the events that will bring to a close history as we know it, followed by the appearance of a new heaven and a new earth.

This, then, is a summary of what John saw and was told to write down. Later we will look at parts of the structure in greater detail, but at least we have an impression of the things that John claims were revealed to him.

John as Listener

EXERCISE 4

Now it is time for you to take a second trip through Revelation. This time, try to discover what John *hears*. In particular, try to identify the voices that speak to him directly. But also pay attention to the other things John hears while he is only a bystander.

The voice that addresses John directly is usually that of the risen Christ. It commands him to write (1:11, 19). It also instructs him not to write down the message of the seven thunders (11:4); instead, it tells him what to do with the second scroll (10:8–11) and to measure the temple (11:1–3). The same voice tells him to "Come up here" into the heavenly throne room (4:1), the same command given to the two witnesses in 11:12. We can assume that the blessing in 14:13 is also spoken by Christ, since it is paired in the next verse with a prophetic saying spoken by the Spirit. The phrase "I am coming soon," which is repeated three times (22:7, 12, and 20), is more of an independent saying or oracle, spoken not just to John but to the churches, as in chapters 2—3. If Christ is also the speaker in 22:13, then the attributes of God as creator apply to Christ as the coming one.

The opening verse of Revelation prepares us for the fact that this message was often delivered to John through divine messengers. Thus it is not surprising that one of the elders speaks to him (7:13–17) and that angels instruct him in many other instances (10:9, 11; 17:1–2, 7–18; 19:9–10; 21:9). In the closing section the speakers are not always identified clearly; but apparently the angel mentioned in 22:1, 8 is also the speaker in 22:6, 10–11. The warning not to change anything in the book (22:18–19) could have been spoken by that same angel, or by Jesus (22:16), although it is certainly a message that John wants his audience to hear and obey.

As a listener, John overhears many things that are not spoken directly to him. In most cases these are announcements or commands delivered by heavenly creatures. These include the four living creatures (6:1–4), an eagle (8:13), and of course angels (7:3; 10:5–7; 14:7–11, 15, 18; 16:1; 19:17–18). Three angels announce the destruction of Babylon in 18:2–3, 4–8, and 21–24. John hears the trumpet blasts in chapters 7—11, as well as voices from the altar (6:14; 16:7) and from the throne (16:17; 19:5; 21:3–8). What John hears includes a long list of doxologies or songs of praise, the prayer or petition by the souls of the martyrs (6:10), and the voices of a heavenly choir (14:2–3).

The striking thing about this list is that virtually all these vocal events occur in, or originate from, a heavenly location. The only earthly speakers are the worshipers of the beast (13:4) and those lamenting the fall of Babylon (18:9–20). For the most part, then, John receives no ordinary communications but messages from a realm beyond our everyday experience. As a charismatic prophet, he claims to relay those messages to his audience and his readers.

John's Other Source

If you have ever read mystery stories or watched them on television, you know there are two different ways in which they are told. In the *Columbo* series, for example, the detective (played by Peter Falk) almost always knew something that we as viewers did not know. He seemed smarter than we were, because he was holding back some secrets. In *Murder, She Wrote,* on the other hand, Jessica Fletcher (played by Angela Lansbury) usually solves the crime by picking up a clue that we all saw but didn't think was important. This can apply to our study of Revelation in two ways.

First, almost everything you have learned so far about John's book has come from your own powers of observation. All the information we have looked for is there in the text, once you know how to find it. Like Jessica Fletcher, all I have done is to direct you to some important clues.

The second point, I am sorry to say, is that John operates much more like Columbo. He has been holding back some important clues. So far, he has given us the impression that everything in the book came to him directly from his charismatic experience. He gives us the impression that if he had recorded it on videotape, we would have seen and heard exactly what he did. What he doesn't tell us, because he doesn't use footnotes, is that most of his symbols and images come from the Bible and other Jewish writings of his time. There are constant allusions to his Bible (our Old Testament), but he never gives us chapter and verse. He expects us to be so immersed in biblical images that we will pick up the clues without his having to explain them. For example, take a minute to read Ezekiel 1:1–3:3 and see whether you don't recognize some of the same imagery you saw in the throne vision (Revelation 4—5) and the command to John to eat the scroll (Revelation 10). Later, when we look at the images of violence in Revelation, we will trace some of them back to their sources.

LITERARY FORMS IN REVELATION

In the final section of this chapter, we need to review the different literary forms that we have already discovered and then to focus on one or two others.

First, we noted that Revelation 2—3 contained seven letters. Actually, these do not fit the typical letter form, either of John's day or of ours. They are really prophetic communications from Christ and the Spirit. In addition to the opening and closing formulas and the words of praise and blame, the letters include other elements that we did not examine: a warning or a threat; words of encouragement; and a different promise in each case to the conqueror(s). The real letter form in Revelation belongs not to these chapters but to the book as a whole. In 1:4–6, John opens his book with an address (from John "to the seven churches that are in Asia") followed by a salutation ("Grace to you and peace"). If you look at the opening of any of Paul's letters, you will find the same format. In 22:8–21 we also find a typical conclusion of a letter as John reminds his readers of the character of his book and ends with a benediction. In other words, John uses this letter form as an envelope to enclose what he saw and heard. The opening and the closing are not unusual, only the content of the letter.

We find a second type of literary form in the *doxologies* or songs of praise that John overhears, such as the "Holy, holy, holy" in 4:8. Many of these are ascriptions of praise: to God (4:8, 11; 7:12; 11:17–18; 16:5–7; 19:1–4); to Christ, usually as the Lamb (5:9–10, 12, 13); and to both (7:10; 11:15; 12:10–12; 15:3–4; 19:6–8). These songs of praise would be natural occasions for the congregations to participate by joining their own voices with those of the heavenly choruses, just as they would join in the closing prayer in 22:20: "Amen. Come, Lord Jesus!"

In the third place, perhaps you noticed a number of what appear to be abrupt announcements that often interrupt the flow of the text. A good example is found in the opening letter: "Look! He is coming with the clouds; every eye will see him, even those who pierced him; and on his account all the tribes of the earth will wail" (1:7). Another appears in 13:9–10, where it is introduced by the phrase "Let anyone who has an ear listen," reminiscent of the Spirit sayings in the letters to the seven churches. In 7:15–17 a similar saying is attributed to an elder, while in 21:3–4 it is announced by a voice from the throne. Nearly all these sayings convey some information about the fate of the listeners. We may refer to the sayings as *oracles* or divine disclosures. We might also include in this category various announcements of Jesus' impending arrival, such as "See, I am coming like a thief!" (16:15) and the three "Surely I am coming soon" sayings which we have already noted in Revelation 22.

A fourth literary form is the *beatitude*. Like the ones in the Sermon on the Mount (Matt. 5:1–12, with a shorter version in Luke 6) and elsewhere, a beatitude begins with the word that is usually translated into English as "blessed" or "happy." The first of these occurs in 1:3: "Blessed is the one who reads aloud the words of the prophecy, and blessed are those who hear and who keep what is written in it." Take a quick look through Revelation and see how

many others you can find. Counting 1:3 as a single blessing, you
should find six others, making a total of seven, which you have already guessed is a favorite number of John's. The blessing on
those who die in the Lord in 14:13 is similar to an oracle, but here
it appears as a saying of Christ himself. Similarly, in 16:15,
"Blessed is the one who stays awake and is clothed" occurs immediately after the oracle about Jesus coming as a thief. The scene is
reminiscent of some of Jesus' sayings and parables about watch-
fulness. In 19:15, the blessing is for those who will participate in
the marriage supper of the Lamb, another echo of one of Jesus'
parables. Also blessed are those who share in the first resurrection
(20:6) and those whose robes are washed (22:14). The final one in
22:7 repeats the theme of 1:3, but again it is linked directly to a
saying about Jesus' coming. All these beatitudes, then, describe
the destiny of the faithful or the behavior expected of them in the
present.

Other forms appear less frequently. The fall of Babylon, as we
have seen, is announced by three angels. Within that context are
three *laments* or dirges, spoken by those human figures who had
profited from trade with the great city: kings (18:9–10), merchants
(18:11–16), shipmasters, seafarers, and sailors (18:17–20).

When we look later at the ethical message of Revelation, we will
pay special attention to *exhortations* such as the ones found in 12:17,
13:9, and 14:12. The sayings sound very much like the letters to the
seven churches, particularly in the call for the endurance of the
saints (the same word translated elsewhere as "patient endurance").
On the other hand, these verses are not attributed to a heavenly figure, so they almost certainly are John's own comments. They emphasize faith and the testimony of Jesus.

CONCLUSION

At this point, I am beginning to feel like a tour guide, and you
probably feel like exhausted tourists. Just think, though, how
much we have learned about John's book just by looking at it
within its own frame of reference. Except for a few instances, we
have not tried to go beyond the book to discover John's sources,
or to explain what his symbols might have meant to his audience,
or to compare and contrast him with other New Testament writers. We will need to make other trips through his book, now that
we have our bearings.

You will no doubt agree that Revelation is a complex book. It is a record of John's experience, but it is also a carefully constructed literary composition using symbols and images from his Jewish heritage. It is indeed a multimedia document.

QUESTIONS FOR DISCUSSION

1. Do you agree that our "second approach" to reading Revelation is different from the usual pattern? What are its advantages and disadvantages?

2. While you were reading Revelation and trying to track John's visions, did you discover a clear pattern, or did you think John was just confused? List questions you would like answered in later chapters of this book.

3. Were you surprised by any of the voices that John heard? Do you think he really heard those voices, or was it just his imagination? If someone today told you the same things, how would you react to that person?

4. Were you surprised by the variety of literary forms in Revelation? Did you notice others that should have been mentioned?

5. Do you think the doxologies or hymns were intended to be sung by the congregations that heard them? Have you heard any of them in worship services?

CHAPTER 3

The People

One of my teachers told of an experience he had as a new, young pastor of a church in rural Tennessee, a part of the country that was not familiar to him. Late one afternoon (or evening, as folks there would say) he visited some parishioners. As time for the evening meal (supper? dinner?) grew closer, he got ready to leave, but the family said "Stay awhile," so he did. The next time he got ready to leave, the same thing happened. Finally, at the third attempt, he decided that he would just have to leave. By the next day, the story was all over town about the preacher who didn't know that "Stay awhile" meant "We enjoyed your visit, but it's time for you to go now."

Now that you have read John's "apocalypse," his written account of what he has seen and heard, you may feel a similar kind of confusion. Many of the characters and scenes seem familiar, such as the stories of the plagues in the book of Exodus, and yet John is using them in very unusual ways. The word "apocalypse," which opens his book, is a signal that he was using a type of literature familiar to his readers but basically mysterious to most of us.

At this point, we do not need to worry about most of the issues that are traditionally covered in a commentary or an introduction to the Revelation/Apocalypse: who John was, when and why he wrote, what kind of persecution if any the churches were facing. Rather, we must try to grope our way into the strange environment he described. We cannot really know what was in John's mind when he wrote these chapters, but the text itself has all the symbols we need for engaging our imagination.

EXERCISE 5

No matter how many times you have read Revelation, read it

again. This time, make a list of the characters who confront you as you read. What do you learn about each of them?

HISTORICAL FIGURES

Revelation is clearly not like most modern novels. The characters are "flat," without any personality development. In fact, many of them are stereotyped figures, like the life-sized cardboard cutouts of celebrities with which you can have your picture taken.

How many actual, historical figures did you find as you read? Certainly the author is one person we can identify—or can we? All that he tells us about himself is that he is on the island of Patmos (1:9), at the eastern end of the Mediterranean; that he has been authorized by God, through Jesus Christ and one of his divine messengers, to write down his visions and send them to these local churches (1:1–3, 9–11; 22:16); that his visions are consistent with the prophetic tradition of the Hebrew Bible and of Jesus (1:3; 19:10; 22:6–9, 18–19). He did *not* claim to be one of the twelve disciples who was a companion during Jesus' ministry, and nothing in his book suggests that he was reporting words that he heard while Jesus was performing that ministry. He did *not* claim to be an apostle (that is, the title used in the book of Acts primarily for one of the Twelve), and he did *not* claim the title of an elder or a bishop, which would give him direct authority over the churches to which he wrote.

A second person mentioned by name is Antipas. He was obviously known at least to the church in Pergamum, and he had died as a "faithful witness" to Jesus Christ (2:13). The word "witness" in Greek is literally *martus*, from which we get our word "martyr." Unfortunately we know nothing else about this person, except that he is the only individual mentioned by name in Revelation who had actually died for his Christian faith.

In the letters to the seven churches in Revelation 2—3, John condemns the followers of three other individuals. It is possible that the Nicolaitans mentioned in 2:6 and 2:16 had some connection with the Nicolaus mentioned in Acts 6:5 as one of the first "Hellenists," that is, a Jewish Christian from a Gentile background chosen to serve tables as a "deacon." The other leaders condemned are Balaam (2:14) and Jezebel (2:20). All three names are symbolic or representative names, referring to groups in the early church to which John was strongly opposed.

We must say the same about the two prophets described in chapter 11 and the pregnant woman in chapter 12. Do the prophets refer to specific individuals, such as Moses and Elijah, or to Peter and Paul? Does the woman refer to Israel, or to Mary, or to the church? The text is not clear, so that we can no longer identify them with any certainty. All symbols carry more than one level of meaning, especially in Revelation. In the same way, these are symbolic or representative characters. The two prophets have some of the qualities of earlier biblical figures; but the mention of their Lord's crucifixion in 11:8 seems to refer to Jerusalem and to identify them as Christians. Indeed, they represent all Christians who will sacrifice themselves for their faith and thus be raised to new life. The woman who gives birth to the Messiah (12:5) reminds us of the Jewish cradle of Christianity, if that is not mixing a metaphor. By the end of that chapter, however, she represents the church. She flees to the wilderness, where she is protected by God, but her children are persecuted by the dragon (12:13–17).

The only other historical figures are presented in generic terms. Each of the churches in chapters 2—3 is praised and/or condemned for different reasons, but the charges are so broad that it is hard to know what it would have been like to be a member of those congregations. For example, what exactly did they do to be accused of losing their first love (2:4) or of being lukewarm (3:15–16)?

Non-Christian groups are also mentioned in very vague terms. We find two references to the "synagogues of Satan" (2:9; 3:9). After the opening of the sixth seal, "the kings of the earth and the great men and the generals and the rich and the strong, and every one, slave and free, hid in the caves and among the rocks of the mountains" in fear of the day of judgment (6:15, RSV). Similarly, after the sixth trumpet, those who were not killed during the plagues refused to repent (9:20–21). The text offers no clues to help identify them as individuals or to characterize them except in terms of their rebellion against God. Similarly, in the final climactic battle in 20:8, Gog and Magog represent the nations at the farthest corners of the earth, a change from Ezekiel 38—39, where Gog is a ruler and Magog his territory.

Revelation, then, does not give us very much help in describing actual historical characters. Most of the names point to types of people rather than to specific individuals.

MYTHICAL FIGURES

By now you have probably discovered that Revelation has a lot in common with fairy tales such as "Goldilocks" or "Hansel and Gretel" or "Cinderella" or "Jack and the Beanstalk." Those worlds are inhabited by all kinds of strange creatures: bears who like oatmeal, a wolf who is a con artist, mice who are transformed into horses, a fearsome giant who lives in the sky. We are used to the same kind of treatment in comic strips that picture animals who not only can talk but can outsmart their owners. The Apocalypse is a kind of fantasy literature, as we have begun to realize.[1]

Many of the characters who appear most frequently in Revelation are mythical figures. In a religious context, this does not mean they are purely fictional or unreal. John's images point to a different dimension of reality. They are larger-than-life figures who populate a world we can visit only with our imagination or, as in John's case, through visions. If we take them literally, the images are unbelievable and lose their power. Don't expect to go to the beach and see crawling out of the water a beast that is like a leopard with a bear's feet and a lion's mouth and that has ten horns and seven heads (13:1–2). Even the shark in *Jaws* couldn't create more terror than that picture. In John's multidimensional universe, that beast is much more than a weird animal. It forces us to think what power might look like when it becomes corrupt and evil. John's images are less concerned with everyday events than with their ultimate meaning.

EXERCISE 6

Read through Revelation again. This time, look for unusual figures that you would not expect to meet in everyday life. These may be part of John's "zoo," or they may be characters who are larger than life. See how many of them you can find.

There are, of course, beasts, which we should expect to find in an apocalyptic book. Although not human, they are essential to the plot because they initiate much of the action. Some of them are easily recognizable, such as the four horses in chapter 6. Others are more bizarre, such as the ones we encounter in our dreams. The four living creatures resemble a lion, an ox, a human, and an eagle, although they each have six wings and are covered with eyes inside and outside (4:6–8). Together, they apparently represent all living things. The Lamb has seven horns and seven eyes; thus he is all-powerful and all-knowing (5:6). The zoo becomes even stranger in chapter 9. First we meet locusts that look like winged horses, who have a human face and a woman's hair, whose teeth are like a lion's, who have scales like the armored breastplates worn by soldiers, and whose tails sting like scorpions (9:3–11). These are hardly the kind of creature you would like to discover in your basement. Next we encounter horses that have heads of a lion, whose tails are like serpents, and who breathe fire and smoke and sulfur (9:17–19) and a beast from the pit (11:7). Later we meet several creatures with seven heads and ten horns: a red dragon (12:3), a beast from the sea (13:3), and a scarlet beast (17:3). The beast from the earth is a little more modestly dressed, with only two horns; but those are important because they make him the earthly and demonic counterpart of the Lamb (13:11). In 17:9–18, John gives us clues to interpreting some of these figures, traditionally taken to refer to the Roman emperors and the city of Rome; but again we must be careful not to be too precise in trying to identify each of the characters. We also encounter the dragon and the beast, along with their prophet, in 16:12–16, where demonic spirits come out from their mouths like frogs and prepare the nations for the final battle between good and evil. Most of these wild animals are a standard feature of the Old Testament and especially of apocalyptic literature, which John has adapted for his own purposes. John is using these images to help us to grasp the power of evil in all its forms. He does not want us to draw a picture of these beasts but rather to use our imaginations to face the reality they represent.

Most of the other mythical figures are presented as *groups* rather than as individual characters. For example, from the very first verse we are presented with an angel; and throughout the book angels are creatures who bridge the gap between heaven and earth. They communicate messages, and often they precipitate the actions that occur on earth. With rare exceptions (e.g., 7:2–3; 10:1–11), the text does not describe these angels. They appear individually, or in groups of seven, or in great multitudes, but we learn almost nothing about them. They are essential to the plot, since they carry the action forward, but they remain basically anonymous.

The heavenly throne room is crowded with other representative figures. They are not flesh-and-blood, this-worldly beings, and we learn almost nothing about them. These groups include: the seven spirits before the throne (1:4; 4:5); the four living creatures (4:6–7); the twenty-four elders (4:4, 10ff.); the souls of those who had been slain (6:9); the 144,000 (7:4; 14:1–5); a great multitude (7:9ff.); the prophets and saints whom God had rewarded (11:18); those who had conquered the beast (15:2). In the closing visions, the new Jerusalem includes kings of the earth (21:24, different from the ones killed in 19:11–21), along with those whose names are written in the book of life (21:27) and those faithful servants who have God's name on their foreheads (22:4). John's message is that his readers should follow the example of these other figures. They should remain faithful and endure so that they might eventually join that great throng worshiping God face to face.

According to John, the universe consisted not only of earthly and heavenly figures but also of a realm "under the earth" (5:13), which we will examine in the next chapter. Nowhere are we given any description of people who inhabited that underworld, although we are introduced to some characters who emerged from there: a beast (11:7) and some of the most bizarre locusts you could ever imagine (9:1–10). "They have as king over them the angel of the bottomless pit; his name in Hebrew is Abaddon, and in Greek he is called Apollyon" (9:11).

MAJOR CHARACTERS

EXERCISE 7

Now that you have met most of the figures in the Apocalypse, stop and think who are the most important actors. We have met them several times, but we have not singled them out. Who are they, and what can you say about them?

The dominant characters in Revelation are clearly God and Jesus (or "Christ" or the Lamb). Like the other mythical figures, they transcend our ordinary experience. From the beginning to the end of Revelation, God appears as the Alpha and the Omega (1:8; 21:6). These are the first and last letters of the Greek alphabet; like our "A to Z," they represent the extent of God's sovereignty. John's major encounter with God is reported in chapter 4, the scene in which John was transported into heaven. The description of a

heavenly vision or a heavenly journey was a typical feature of apocalyptic literature. In John's account, God is not a friendly character like George Burns with a cigar. In fact, there is no description
at all, only a collage of symbols meant to create a sense of awe as
we read what John saw and heard. The figure on the throne cre-
ates the sensation of overwhelming power and authority. We are
meant to feel the way Dorothy and her friends felt when they first
met the Wizard of Oz. Throughout Revelation, God is presented
as the Lord of heaven and earth (e.g., 11:4, 13, 15). God is the
"almighty one" (*pantokratōr* in Greek) and the all-powerful creator
(14:7). God is the receipient of worship, both in heaven and on
earth (e.g., Revelation 4; 14; 15; 19), passages that we will examine
in more detail later. God is the father of the Lamb (14:1), although
that does not necessarily make God a ram. There is a frequent emphasis on the wrath of God and on God's judgment, themes that
we will also explore more carefully in later chapters.

The other central character, of course, is the risen Christ. It is
interesting that the title "Jesus Christ" appears only in the opening
chapter of Revelation, although one passage refers to "the kingdom
of our Lord and of his Christ" (11:15; see also 12:10). The term
"Christ," of course, was originally a title, not a name; it is the Greek
translation of the Hebrew term "Messiah," and this is the way in
which it usually appears in Revelation (20:4, 6). The phrase "Son
of God" appears only in 2:18. In Revelation 4—20, the central
chapters, he is simply called Jesus (e.g., 12:17; 14:12; 17:6; 19:10;
20:4), while in the closing prayer and benediction he is addressed
as "Lord Jesus" (22:20–21; note also the passage about the two
prophets in 11:8 where he is referred to as "their Lord"). In John's
initial vision (1:12–20), which is a counterpart to his vision of God
in Revelation 4, Jesus is described as "one like the Son of Man."
The same term is used again in 14:14, where it is clearly a reference to a final judgment scene; but what is surprising is that a few
verses later the same figure is described as "another angel" (14:17).
If that is in fact another reference to Christ, as it appears to be, then
it pictures him as "a little higher than the angels." As the drama of
the Apocalypse draws to a close, titles originally used for God are
applied to Jesus as well; he is "Lord of lords and King of kings"
(17:14, and again in 19:16 with the titles in the reverse order). In
the final visions in chapters 21—22, he shares the throne with God;
together they symbolize God's presence so that a temple is no
longer necessary; and he too is the Alpha and the Omega (22:13).

Three main images or themes are associated with the risen Lord, which we need to notice only briefly since we will return to them. First, he is the Lamb who has been slain but who now rules. This image is introduced in chapter 5 and then is used throughout the rest of the book. Second, there is a constant emphasis on the fact that he has conquered (e.g., 3:21); he is the real "ruler of the kings of the earth" (1:5) and the "King of kings." Of course, there are battles still to be fought, but he will emerge victorious. Finally, there is a repeated reference to *his coming*. John's salutation to the churches includes the statement, "Look! He is coming with the clouds" (1:7). In the letters to the individual churches in chapters 2—3, his coming is often used as a threat to encourage them to remain obedient (2:5, 16, 25; 3:11); he will come unexpectedly, like a thief (3:5), a theme familiar from the first three Gospels. His coming may be seen as a day of wrath (e.g., 6:16–17), although to the worshipers nothing could be more fitting than the closing prayer: "Amen. Come, Lord Jesus!" (22:20).[2]

UNSEEN CHARACTERS

So far, we have looked at the characters who are actually mentioned in the Apocalypse. We need to remember, however, that the text has other people in mind, the different audiences to which Revelation was addressed. The term "audience" is itself intriguing, since it implies hearing rather than reading. You remember that one of the opening verses gives quite explicit instructions about this: "Blessed is the one who reads aloud the words of the prophecy, and blessed are those who hear and who keep what is written in it" (1:3). We noticed that this is a "blessing" or "beatitude." John's churches did not have books or duplicating machines or printers. They had no pew Bibles; and even if they had, most of the people could not read. Therefore the Apocalypse was meant to be read out loud, probably during a worship service. The instructions in this verse are directed to both the reader and the listeners, in both cases encouraging them to shape their lives by the visions and the message in the book. Although the Apocalypse was obviously written to churches in a different time and place, we cannot help reading it from the perspective of our own time and place. Therefore we too become part of the audience, whether we like it or not.

QUESTIONS FOR DISCUSSION

1. Revelation is very different from the book of Acts, which describes real church leaders with whom people can identify as role models or heroes. Which do you find more effective? Why?

2. Some Christians in Ephesus and Pergamum and Thyatira receive a really harsh rebuke. Did they deserve it? What had they done wrong?

3. We only sampled the images John uses to describe God and Christ. What other images found in Revelation would you add to the list? Are there other important images that you think John should have included?

4. Do you agree that John's symbolic language (his images) should not be taken literally but rather as pointers to the deeper meaning of human life and history? Which ones, if any, would you interpret literally?

CHAPTER 4

The Places

In an earlier chapter, I suggested taking a quick walk through the Apocalypse in order to get an overview of the territory. Now I would like to suggest a different approach. Pretend to be a detective; anyone who reads a book should be one! Look for clues that will help you to understand John's peculiar message. Since you already know something about John's style and plot and characters, look for other details that will help you to unravel his message.

JOHN'S MULTIDIMENSIONAL VIEW OF REALITY

As you have already discovered, John's view of reality is multidimensional. Temporally, he sees current events from the perspective of the God "who is and was and is to come." Spatially, he sees things happening in three dimensions: in heaven, on earth, and from the underworld.

EXERCISE 8

Your assignment, should you choose to accept it, is to look through Revelation and see what you can discover about each of the three places just mentioned (heaven, earth, and the pit). Who is there? What happens there?

Heaven, according to John, is God's permanent residence, a fact that comes as no real surprise. That view does not exclude God from human affairs; it means only that God is much greater than our ordinary experience and understanding. In addition to God, other individuals who are identified in heaven are the Lamb and Michael, a leader of the angels in the war against Satan (11:7–9). There are also the characters whom we have already identified: the four living creatures, the twenty-four elders, various angels, the 144,000, a great multitude, the souls of the slain, and those who have conquered the beast (15:2). Heaven is a place of glory—both in its original meaning of the presence of God and also in the sense of the praise that is continually being given to God. It is also a place of peace, following the expulsion of "the Devil and Satan" just mentioned.

Earth, on the other hand, is a place of conflict. It is the place where the plagues occur. It is where Balaam and Jezebel and the Nicolaitans and the "synagogue of Satan" threaten the churches. It is where the two prophets are killed, the woman and her child are harassed, the two beasts demand total allegiance, and the demonic spirits encourage the kings of the earth to wage a climactic battle against the forces of good (16:13 and 19:19). From above, the dragon is thrown down from heaven and attacks the woman, and conflict is predicted (12:12); yet it is surprising that the earth comes to her protection (12:13–16). From below, the locusts released from the pit (9:1–11) torture people for five months, and two beasts arise from the sea and the earth. In John's view, the earth is where we live, where our loyalty to God and the Lamb is constantly being questioned, and where we have to make life-and-death decisions. It is a place of conflict.

The underworld is the third dimension of John's topography. This place is the location of the "bottomless pit," which is the source of much of the world's evil (9:2, 11; 17:8; 20:1). Apparently the underworld also contains the "lake of fire" (19:20; 20:14; 21:8). As such, it represents eternal damnation, that is, separation from God.

John's basic view of the universe, then, reflects a battle between good and evil on a cosmic scale.

THE NATURAL ENVIRONMENT

EXERCISE 9

Now look for other aspects of John's view of the universe. For the time being, you can ignore the chapters that deal with the plagues (chapters 6—11 and 17). They deal with natural disasters, and we will study them later. Instead, look for other features of John's environment and ask yourself whether they play a positive or a negative role. Are they basically good or evil?

The first feature we meet in Revelation is seven *stars*. John explains that these stars are the angels of the seven churches (1:20; 2:1; 3:1). Some interpreters think the stars refer to leaders of the local congregations. However, John never uses ordinary New Testament terms for leaders (such as deacon or elder or bishop); and everywhere else in Revelation "angel" refers to a heavenly messenger. It is much more likely that when John writes to the "angels" of these churches, he means something like guardian angels. Note also that Christ promises the church in Thyatira the morning star (2:28). Stars also appear in the plagues, as we shall see, along with other celestial bodies.

On the other hand, the *sea* almost always has a negative connotation. In 12:12, a woe (the opposite of a beatitude or blessing) tells us that the descent of the devil from heaven means conflict on earth. In 13:1–2, the beast that emerges from the sea recalls an ancient Near Eastern myth that the sea symbolizes chaos, which can be controlled only by God's creative and providential actions.[1] If you have ever lived near the seashore during a hurricane or a severe storm, you know how destructive the ocean can be when it is angry. As I write this, I am looking at a photograph of a fifty-foot boat that carried me through the eye of a hurricane. On the wall to my left is a photograph (taken in 1903, believe it or not!) of a sailing ship taken from the deck of another ship. The one in the distance has all its sails furled, and separating the two ships is a wave that must be at least forty feet high. The sea has always been a dangerous place, so John uses it as a traditional symbol of chaos and destruction. Since sea travel was so dangerous, it is not surprising that at the final resurrection John specifically mentions those who were lost at sea (20:13). On the whole, then, the sea is a symbol of the conflict between good and evil that is at the heart of John's message. Exceptions to that statement are the references to the "sea of glass" mentioned in 4:6 and 15:2 (where it is "mixed with fire"). We cannot tell its precise function in John's celestial vision, but it may also be an allusion to a gigantic bowl, holding ten thousand gallons of water, which stood in the courtyard of the original Solomonic temple in Jerusalem. This "sea" may also reflect the ancient myth. In other words, it may symbolize God's ability to create order out of chaos. That message would have been more understandable to John's original readers than it is to us today.

Similar to the sea is a *river*. In 12:15, the serpent spews out a torrent of water in order to drown the woman who represents the church, but the earth comes to her rescue. The river also has a menacing aspect in two specific references to the Euphrates, the great river that flowed through the city of Babylon. The first mention in 9:14 precedes an invasion of 200 million troops. The second time it is mentioned (16:12) the river dries up and allows kings from further east to invade. The river, then, is another symbol of destruction.

A symbol that has a variety of meanings is the *wilderness*. The origin of this image, of course, is the forty years the people of Israel spent wandering between the time they left Egypt and when they entered the land of Canaan. The first three Gospels report that Jesus followed a similar pattern by retreating into the wilderness for forty days before his active ministry. In Revelation, the wilderness functions positively as a place of protection for the woman who represents the church (12:6, 14); but on the other hand, it is also the location of the whore called Babylon, the woman sitting on a scarlet beast (17:3–6). In John's view, then, the wilderness is a place of security, but also a source of evil.

Mountains also play an important role in John's visions. In one of the plagues symbolized by trumpets, an apparently volcanic mountain is thrown into the sea (8:8). Mount Zion is mentioned in 14:1. Historically, this was the place where the temple in Jerusalem was located. It was also the place where Christ's return was expected. In sharp contrast is the city of Rome, located on seven hills or mountains (17:9). It confronted John's listeners with the major challenge to their faith. We can see, then, that mountains play both a positive and a negative role in John's visions. On the negative side, John expected the final battle between the heavenly and the demonic forces to occur at Armageddon (16:16). That is not the name of any place known to us, but John's attempt at a Hebrew derivation suggests the "hill" of Megiddo. It was a place in the northern part of Israel that controlled the trade routes. It was also the site of famous battles, especially the one celebrated in the Song of Deborah (Judges 5). However, when John actually describes the battle in 19:17–21, he does not bother to mention the location. Equally ambiguous are the names Gog and Magog (20:7). John seems to assume that they represent the nations that will be present at the final battle between good and evil. Unfortunately they are on the losing side.

Finally, we should not lose sight of the fact that the final scene is a *garden*. In the heavenly city, there is a river of life (a positive meaning) and the tree of life. Eden has returned; paradise is regained.

CITIES

EXERCISE 10

Now take a look at the cities that are mentioned in Revelation. What does John say about them? Is he talking about identifiable cities, such as Los Angeles and Boston, or do they have much more symbolic content?

The first place mentioned in Revelation is Patmos (1:9), which is not a city but an island located in the Mediterranean just off the coast of Asia Minor, or what is known today as Turkey. He tells us nothing about this location except his reason for being there.

Immediately after that, he mentions the seven cities in Asia Minor to which he is sending this letter (1:11, the same ones mentioned in chapters 2—3). A brief look at the map of that area shows you that these cities are arranged in a sort of circle. They were connected by a good road system, so that may have been an ancient postal route. As a result of recent historical and archaeological investigations we know quite a bit about those cities.[2] However, John tells us very little about them since his focus is on the churches.

The next places mentioned by name are Sodom and Egypt (11:8). In the Old Testament, Sodom was the epitome of corruption. Egypt, although not a city, was the place where the people of Israel were slaves. John makes it clear that he is not referring to those ancient places. For one thing, he qualifies the names by saying that he is speaking spiritually, a term also translated as "prophetically" (NRSV), or "allegorically" (RSV), or "figuratively" (NIV). He also refers to them as the place where "their Lord was crucified." This suggests that Jerusalem was a corrupt and evil city because it was the place where Jesus was crucified, but it can also be a metaphor for Rome. In other words, John does not expect the place names to be taken literally.

John's use of metaphor becomes even clearer in the references to Babylon, whose destruction is predicted in 14:8 and described in chapters 17—18. Years earlier, in 587 B.C.E., a Babylonian army

had destroyed the city of Jerusalem and its temple. For that reason, in the Jewish tradition the name Babylon came to symbolize
the embodiment of evil. John continues that tradition when he describes Babylon as a prostitute who has seduced other world leaders (17:1–5) and as a woman "drunk with the blood of the saints
and the blood of the witnesses to Jesus" (17:6). In the verses that
follow (17:9–11), the fluidity of John's images is apparent when he
identifies the woman/beast as both seven mountains and seven
kings at the same time. His original hearers would immediately
have understood these to refer to the city of Rome (the city on
seven hills) and to Roman emperors, even though the identity of
individual emperors in 17:10 is still a matter of debate. The ruin
of the city is described in chapter 18 in a series of dirges: the first
two spoken by angelic or heavenly voices, the next three by kings
and merchants and seafarers, and the last by a third angel. The
chorus in 19:1–8 celebrates the victory over the source of all evil.

In obvious contrast to Babylon, in 19:6–8 there is an announcement of a wedding to take place in the near future between
the Lamb and his bride, and in the next verse the prophet John is
actually instructed to send out the wedding invitations. Yet once
the bride appears in chapter 21, she has been transformed into a
city, the new Jerusalem (21:2). From this transition, we can see
clearly that the Apocalypse does not make any sharp distinction
between people and places. Revelation describes events in the
fluid kind of language we usually associate with cartoons. Just as
the U.S.S.R. was usually pictured as a bear, and Uncle Sam as an
old man with a top hat, so Revelation contrasts a lady of the night
with a new bride and a city of corruption with one of perfection.

ARCHITECTURE

EXERCISE 11

If you are still in the detective mode, ask yourself what buildings
and other objects occupy John's landscape and heavenscape.

Two objects dominate the heavenly scene: the temple (a place of
worship) and a throne (a seat of authority). John may be referring to
the Holy of Holies, the most sacred part of the Jerusalem temple

where God was symbolically enthroned (16:17). The *temple*, for John, is the setting for the continual praise and worship of God. In a series of visions John discloses more and more features of that temple: an altar (6:9; 8:3; 9:13); the ark of the covenant (11:19); and "the temple of the tent of witness" (15:5). That last phrase is awkward, but it apparently refers to the tabernacle, the portable sanctuary that was carried by the Israelites during the sojourn in the wilderness. It housed the ark, the portable throne of God. Significantly, in the new Jerusalem there is no temple (21:22). There is no need for one, since God and the Lamb are fully present to those who worship them.

In one curious passage, John is told to measure "the temple of God and the altar and those who worship there" (11:1–2). Some interpreters take this to be the earthly temple in Jerusalem, although it was probably in ruins at the time when John was writing, having been destroyed by Roman troops in 66–70 C.E. in a war to suppress Jewish revolutionaries. More likely it refers to the heavenly sanctuary and represents all those who are faithful worshipers of God and the Lamb.

John refers to God's throne nearly forty times in almost every chapter of his book, especially in those chapters where God is being praised (e.g., chapters 4—5 and 7). At the last judgment it is identified as a great white throne (20:11). It is the ultimate symbol of God's power. For that reason, we should not miss the significance of the transfer of that power to Christ. In the message to the Laodiceans, Christ promises to share his throne with those who conquer, just as he shares the throne with the Father (3:21); and in the final scene in the holy city there is only one throne, that of God and the Lamb (22:3).

On earth, the dragon gives to the beast from the sea "his power and his throne and great authority" (13:2). From John's perspective such authority is really a pretense. It can threaten Christians with imprisonment (2:10). It can create conflict and wars, but the power of the "kings of the earth" is limited. It cannot win out in the long run.

QUESTIONS FOR DISCUSSION

1. Is the message of Revelation antiurban? In other words, does it represent cities as being inherently corrupt?

2. If heaven is portrayed as a place of peace and earth as a place of conflict, where would you rather be? Why?

3. In our modern scientific generation, we still tend to think of our globe as a rare, perhaps unique, place to support human life. The rest of the universe seems rather hostile. What do you think is the "real" world for John? Where is it located?

Images of Conflict in Revelation

CHAPTER 5

The Dimensions
of Conflict

In part 1, we explored John's multidimensional view of reality
and the plot of his book. We met a cast of stereotyped characters:
historical and mythical, heroes and villains. We looked at the
many symbolic places that occupy John's universe. Again and
again, we had to conclude that Revelation shows us a world in conflict, ultimately a moral conflict between good and evil. In the next
set of chapters we will focus on the images John uses to describe
that moral conflict.

CONFLICT WITHIN THE CHURCH

EXERCISE 12

Read again Revelation 2—3, the letters that John sent to the angels of the seven churches. They give at least a glimpse of what the
people in those churches had to face. As you read, look for the formula in each of the letters (or look at the discussion above in chapter 2). Then identify the problems that those Christians were facing. In chapter 15 below, we will ask what the letters tell them
about how they should live.

Even though the Greek word for "church" (*ekklēsia*) is used
only in Revelation 1—3 and in 22:16, Christians are always the focus of John's attention. Not just the letters but the entire book was
to be read to those churches (1:3). On the other hand, we should
not assume that John was writing to all the churches in those seven
cities but only to congregations that acknowledged his charismatic

authority. They did not have permanent houses of worship. Rather, they met in people's homes or possibly in some public place where they would be safe.

The formula or pattern in each of the letters, as you recall, begins "To the angel of the church in . . . write." Then comes "These are the words," followed by a phrase or an image of the risen Christ drawn from the opening vision in Revelation 1. In each letter, the phrase "I know" indicates Christ's awareness of the life of the congregation. That is followed by words of praise and/or blame and then either a call to repentance or a word of encouragement. At the conclusion of the letter, although not always in the same sequence, is a word promising a gift to those who conquer and a word of advice: "Let anyone who has an ear listen to what the Spirit is saying to the churches." The gifts or promises are important, since they are mentioned again in the closing chapters of his book.

We do not have to read far to discover that the first dimension of conflict is within the churches. There are at least two related issues.

1. First, there is a conflict over leadership and authority. The Ephesian church is praised for having rejected false apostles (2:3), and later it is also commended because it hates "the works of the Nicolaitans, which I also hate" (2:6). Even though John claims to be speaking the words of Christ (or the Spirit), we have to feel that he shares the same opinion.

In virtually every other instance in the New Testament, "apostle" refers either to one of Jesus' inner circle of disciples (the Twelve) or to traveling evangelists like Paul, who had no permanent congregation. We can assume that the ones mentioned in Ephesus were also outsiders and not resident pastors. The only other references to apostles in Revelation are so general that they give us no new information.[1] We can only conjecture who these apostles were and what they taught.

On the other hand, we get the impression that the Nicolaitans in Ephesus (2:6) and in Pergamum (2:15), along with Balaam in Pergamum (2:14) and Jezebel in Thyatira (2:20), are local church leaders. John even admits that Jezebel was a female prophet, possibly representing a challenge to John's own prophetic authority. Revelation was written to warn Christians to reject the position of those other church leaders. Thus it reflects a conflict over the direction in which the churches should grow. From every indication, the crisis was not about doctrine or orthodox teaching, in contrast to other New Testament writings such as 1 and 2 John and the Pastoral letters. In Revelation, the issue is not theology but practice.

2. The real disagreement over an appropriate Christian lifestyle focused on two specific issues: whether or not to "eat food sacrificed to idols" and to "practice fornication." The terms are used in this sequence in 2:14 (applying to Balaam) and in the reverse order in 2:20 (applied to Jezebel).

As we noted earlier, these two names are symbolic. John has drawn them from the Hebrew Bible, where the names are associated with these two issues. Numbers 25:1–2 reports that some Israelites began sleeping with foreign (Moabite) women. The women then seduced the Israelites into idolatry. "These invited the people to the sacrifices of their gods, and the people ate and bowed down to their gods." In Numbers 31:16 this event is blamed on Balaam's advice. Similarly, Jezebel refers to the wife of King Ahab of Israel, who convinced her husband to promote the worship of the local Baal cult (1 Kings 16:31–33), presumably with its practice of sacred prostitution; and she is portrayed as being responsible for the killing of Israelite prophets (1 Kings 18:4, 13).

Eating food offered to idols was a kind of test case for Jews and Christians, who did not recognize the existence of other gods. In Pergamum and Thyatira, as well as in the other cities of Asia Minor, Christians were confronted all the time with the worship of other gods and goddesses. It was perfectly acceptable to be eclectic and to worship at more than one temple. At some, sacred meals were held. Also, the meat sold in the marketplace was almost certainly from an animal that had been sacrificed or dedicated to one of the other deities. The message of Revelation is that Christians should avoid using such food at all costs. There should be no compromise with idolatry.

At an earlier time, Paul dealt with the same issue in response to a question addressed to him by Christians in Corinth. In 1 Corinthians 8 and again in 10:1–22, he admitted that it would be all right to eat at sacred meals in the temples so long as they had the "knowledge" that idols do not really exist. Similarly, they were free to eat meat at home (10:23–30). It was a matter of conscience. In both cases, though, he advised against such behavior if it would undermine the faith of some who were "weak." Paul's more moderate position, apparently, was close to that of the Nicolaitans and Balaam and Jezebel. For that reason, it is tempting to identify

"Jezebel" with Lydia, a native of Thyatira who was converted by Paul in Philippi (Acts 16:14–15); but to do so would be speculation or historical fiction. From Paul's point of view, John's churches would fall among the "weak." From their point of view, however, any compromise with the pagan cults would constitute idolatry. The conflict was over the question of where to draw the line.

The second issue is even more complicated because it is hard to know how to interpret the Greek verb *porneuein*. The traditional translation has been "to commit fornication," although many people today are not too sure what that means. The RSV adopts the more neutral phrase "practice immorality," which ignores the sexual overtones of the Greek verb; similar translations suggest "immoral practices" (Goodspeed) or "immorality" (Massyngberde Ford). Probably the most accurate is "sexual immorality" (NIV). But what exactly was the problem? There are three most likely interpretations. One is that some local temples had a ritual of sexual intercourse that allowed worshipers to engage in a symbolic sacred marriage. That takes the term literally; but there is no hard evidence for such a ritual at that time. A second possibility is that *porneuein* referred to sexual license in a much broader sense, as it was practiced in some later Gnostic sects. Such Christians claimed that, since they had been freed from the bondage of the flesh, they were able to do whatever they wanted to do.[2] A third interpretation recognizes that "fornication" or "sexual immorality," like prostitution, was used as a metaphor for idolatry, especially in the Hebrew Bible. It did not mean explicit sexual behavior, but rather being unfaithful to God. This interpretation is the most likely, since all the leading characters are so highly symbolic. Even in 1 Kings, Jezebel was never condemned for literally being an adulteress. The real temptation for Christians in Asia Minor was to participate in worship at some of the local temples. John, speaking for Christ, condemned any such compromise. He threatened Jezebel with the equivalent of AIDS, which would infect and kill any of her followers. Within the symbolic world of Revelation, the false leaders threatened the integrity and purity of the church.

A CONFLICT OF
RELIGIOUS LOYALTIES

Early Christians soon found their new faith under attack from more than one direction. The book of Revelation encourages them to remain steadfast, no matter what the cost. We can see evidence of that conflict in the letters to the seven churches.

1. On the one hand, Christians had to defend their faith in Jesus as the Messiah from attack by Jews. Christianity emerged as a prophetic movement within Judaism. Only gradually, especially after the Jewish War of 66–70 C.E., was it recognized as a new religion. One of the burning issues in the first Christian century was a conflict with the synagogues over which tradition was the true successor of Israel and which tradition read the Hebrew Bible correctly. That theme is particularly evident in Paul's letters to the Romans and the Galatians, in Matthew's Gospel, and in Hebrews. The book of Acts gives a number of stylized examples of ways in which such conflicts broke out in public. So we should not be surprised to find references to the "synagogue of Satan" in John's letters to Smyrna (2:9) and Philadelphia (3:9). Both are references to "those who say that they are Jews and are not." It is possible that these statements apply to apostate Jews, that is, ones who had assimilated into the culture like the followers of Balaam and Jezebel whom John criticizes. But why would they interest John? The more obvious explanation is that these were Jews who refused to accept Jesus as Lord and Christ (Messiah). In Smyrna, John says, Christians were being slandered by those "false" Jews (2:9); and Christ promises the church in Philadelphia that he "will make them come and bow down before your feet, and they will learn that I have loved you" (3:9). The passages are not anti-Semitic, but they do reflect a very real clash of religious loyalties.

2. Just as obviously, the early Christians had to defend their new faith from the temptations of polytheism. We can assume that many Christians in John's seven churches, like many of Paul's converts, came from a Gentile background. That does not mean they had been "pagans," in the sense of being nonreligious. As we have noted, it was possible to belong to more than one civic group and also to attend temples dedicated to more than one deity, where the main activity was to offer sacrifices. Such temples were part of the religious culture in each of the seven cities. John's warning against eating food offered to idols and against sexual immorality (idolatry) shows that dealing with this polytheistic environment must have been a real struggle for many in John's audience. Other temptations included magic, astrology, and various forms of popular superstition. In this hostile setting John praised their past faithfulness, and he also warned them against any kind of accommodation.

3. The references to "Satan's throne" and "the place where Satan lives" in the letter to Pergamum (2:13) point to an even more difficult challenge: the imperial cult. Throughout the first century C.E., the Roman emperors were increasingly treated as divine figures: the first emperors after their death, later ones during their lifetime. In some of the seven cities of Revelation there were actual temples to the emperor and to the goddess Roma, protector of the eternal city. Pergamum had the first such temple in Asia Minor. In other cities, the worship of the emperor was often linked to various deities in the form of statues in their temples. Frequent festivals reinforced the cult. Loyalty to the emperor, and to the empire that he represented, took the form of religious devotion.[3] "Satan's throne" suggests just this blending of religious and secular power, an ironic contrast to God's throne. Christians were increasingly faced with a dilemma: to participate in the imperial cult and be regarded as good citizens, or to refuse to participate because the worship of the emperor was another form of idolatry. By the early part of the second century C.E., as we know from a letter from Pliny the Younger (governor of the neighboring province of Bithynia) to the then emperor Trajan, Christians who refused to worship the emperor were put to death. John is aware that Christians who refuse may ultimately have to pay that price.

A CONFLICT BETWEEN
CHURCH AND EMPIRE

Rome used religion to reinforce the power of the empire. Not only did the emperor cult serve this function, but Rome determined which religions (and civic associations) would be permitted to function. Judaism was not recognized as a legitimate religion, but Jews were given religious freedom as long as they did not challenge Roman authority and paid their taxes. Once Christianity emerged from the protected status of Judaism and became recognized as a new religion, then it was subject to persecution by the state. Therefore, for Christians to resist Roman religion was, implicitly or explicitly, a challenge to the social, political, and economic power of the empire.

EXERCISE 13

So far, we have concentrated on issues in the letters to the seven churches. Now we need to look to other sections of the Apocalypse to see whether the issue of idolatry surfaces there as well. Read especially chapters 13 (the two beasts) and 17—18 (the fall of Babylon). Do you see any other evidence that Christians saw themselves in conflict with the power of the empire?

The most frequent and most convincing intepretation of the two beasts is that they are images of the Roman Empire in both of its aspects. The beast from the sea stands for the total religious-secular power of the state. The dragon (Satan) gives this beast "his power and his throne and great authority" (13:2). The whole earth follows the beast (13:3), accepts its authority (13:7), and worships it (13:8) just as it does the dragon (13:4). The beast dares to challenge God (13:6) and make war on the saints (13:7). That last verse makes the church-state conflict absolutely clear. When John gives his interpretation of the beast, we know that this total power is embodied, at least temporarily, in the particular "kings" or emperors (17:9–11). What about the second beast, the one from the earth? A clue is found in the statement, "It makes the earth and its inhabitants worship the first beast" (13:12), an apparent reference to the priesthood of the imperial cult. There may even be a veiled sarcastic allusion in 13:15: "so that the image of the beast could even speak." At Ephesus there was a huge statue of Zeus. The priests could climb into it and become the voice of the statue, a prototype of the Wizard of Oz.

A second symbol of idolatry is Babylon, the prostitute in chapters 17—18. She is the antitype or counterpart, both to the woman threatened by the dragon (chapter 12) and to the bride of Christ (19:9; 21:9). John is not a misogynist or an antifeminist here.[4] It is unfortunately true that images of seduction tend to be female. However, John is simply using a stock image from his Bible and other Jewish literature, well known to his audience, so that he can hardly be blamed for not having a modern conscience. His concern was to illuminate what happens to those who deny their loyalty to the one true God. The woman is mysterious (17:5). She is not identical with the beast on whose seven heads she sits (17:9), although John identifies her as the city "that rules over the kings of the earth" (17:18). That meant Rome, although by extension it can also refer to any temporal power that persecutes Christians. The fact that she was "drunk with the blood of the saints and the blood of the martyrs of Jesus" (17:6, RSV; cf. 18:24) recalls Nero's ruthless treatment of the Christians in the middle sixties of the first century. The charge against her is that the kings of the earth have committed fornication with her (17:2; 18:3, 9). Since that cannot be meant literally, it reinforces our view that "fornication" is a symbol for idolatry. Babylon epitomizes all those worldly powers that reject God and engage in conflict with the church.

In this chapter, then, we have identified at least three dimensions of conflict. First, churches may be divided over how to behave in a culture that is hostile to them. Second, people who remain faithful to the God revealed in Jesus Christ may find themselves in conflict with people holding other religious beliefs. Third, when the secular power of a military regime or a drug cartel or a multinational corporation tries to become a substitute for the power of God, Christians may find themselves in conflict. Still, we have not penetrated to the deepest dimension of conflict in Revelation—a cosmic conflict between the powers of good and evil. That will concern us in the next few chapters.

QUESTIONS FOR DISCUSSION

1. For many early Christians, whether or not to eat food offered to idols was a test case of their total loyalty to the one true God. Would you have sided with those Corinthian Christians who saw nothing wrong with doing it, with Paul's mediating position, or with John's refusal to have anything to do with it? Why?

2. What issues today do you think test our loyalty to God in the same way that the early Christians were tested?

3. How is the church different from other organizations that offer fellowship, service, and a sense of belonging—for example, Kiwanis or the PTA or Alcoholics Anonymous?

4. In ancient Rome, religion was intended to reinforce loyalty to the empire. In Colonial America, most of the colonies had an established church for the same reason. With the separation of church and state guaranteed by our Constitution, do you think we have gone too far in the other direction?

CHAPTER 6

Images Of
Natural Catastrophes

Natural disasters fascinate us. The latest tornado or hurricane or flood or earthquake may dominate the news for days or weeks, even if it is not in our local area. We are horrified by the destruction and loss of life and property. We identify with those who have lost loved ones. The question "Why does God allow human suffering?" is perhaps hardest to answer when we are dealing with natural catastrophes, since they are beyond our control. Yet major sections of Revelation deal with just such disasters. We will look first at the plagues (and at some passages that may have influenced John) and at two similar passages before we explore their meaning.

THE PLAGUES

EXERCISE 14

Read again the two sets of seven (trumpets and bowls) that we usually call the plagues: Revelation 8:6–11:19 and chapters 15—16. In each case, make a list of the sequence of events. As each trumpet is blown or bowl poured out, what happens? Who is affected? Then read the set of seven seals (6:1–8:5). See how the three sets are alike and how are they different.

You probably noticed that the last two sets, the trumpets and the bowls, are very similar. In each case, if we ask, "What causes the disaster?" then we see the following sequence.

Trumpet visions. (1) Hail and fire, mixed with blood, are thrown to earth; (2) something like a volcanic mountain is thrown into the sea; (3) a great star called Wormwood falls into the rivers and springs; (4) sun, moon, and stars are struck, although we are not told how; (5) a star, fallen to earth, unlocks the pit and allows rather unusual locusts to escape; (6) four angels at the Euphrates are released and apparently lead an army of 200 million, whose horses breathe fire and smoke and sulfur; (7) there are songs of praise in heaven but no plague until the heavenly temple is opened. Then there are "flashes of lightning, rumblings, peals of thunder, an earthquake, and heavy hail" (11:19).

Bowl Visions. (1) On earth, people are afflicted with sores or boils; (2) the sea is turned to blood; (3) rivers and springs also turn bloody; (4) the sun scorches people; (5) the beast's throne is the target and his kingdom is thrown into darkness; (6) the Euphrates dries up and three demonic spirits in the shape of frogs assemble the kings of the world for a final battle; (7) a voice from the throne announces the end of the plagues. That is followed by "flashes of lightning, rumblings, peals of thunder," an earthquake of unprecedented magnitude which destroys Babylon, and enormous hailstones (16:18–21).

With the exception of the fifth plague, the sequences are strikingly similar: earth, sea, fresh waters, sun and/or heavenly bodies, armies from the Euphrates or beyond, and voices in heaven. The fifth plague, in different ways, pictures the agony of those without the seal of God, in other words the followers of the beast.

Now if we ask "Who or what is affected by each plague, and how extensive is the damage?" we get the following answers.

Trumpet Visions. (1) A third of the earth and trees are destroyed, along with all grass; (2) a third of all sea creatures and a third of all ships are lost; (3) many people die from drinking the bitter water; (4) the amount of light, during both the day and the night, is reduced by a third; (5) people without God's seal are tortured by the locusts for five months; (6) a third of humanity is killed by the fire, smoke, and sulfur coming from the horses' mouths.

Bowl Visions. (1) Apparently all who have the mark of the beast suffer painful sores; (2) everything in the sea dies; (3) no indication of the result, except that God is praised for acting justly; (4) followers of the beast are scorched with fire from the sun; (5) they curse God because of their pains and sores; (6) the troops assemble at Harmagedon (or Armageddon), but the battle does not yet occur. Incidentally, the angel's song of praise in 16:6 and the response from the altar in the next verse answer the question asked by the martyrs in 6:10: "Sovereign Lord, holy and true, how long will it be before you judge and avenge our blood on the inhabitants of the earth?"

THE SEVEN SEALS

If we turn to the seven seals (6:1–8:5), two things are immediately obvious. First, the sequence of events is quite different, particularly when the first four seals are opened. In fact, these are not plagues at all. Except for the sequel to the opening of the sixth seal (6:12–17), the disasters occur as the result of human violence rather than from purely natural causes. Second, the structure of this set of visions is much closer to the trumpet sequence than either one is to the bowl visions. In both the seal and the trumpet cycles the first four actions are stated with almost no elaboration, whereas the fifth and the sixth are rather complex. Also, both cycles have a long interruption or an interlude between the sixth and the seventh steps.

Keep in mind that in this set of visions the heavenly scroll, introduced in Revelation 5, is not actually opened. Since it is rolled up, the message written inside—presumably the message that John is to deliver to the churches—cannot be read. The scroll is closed with not just one but seven separate wax seals, guaranteeing its secrecy. As each seal is broken, a different calamity occurs. In the case of the first four, a different-colored horse appears; together they are the infamous "four horsemen of the Apocalypse." The last three of those are self-explanatory: red = war, black = famine, pale green = death (and Hades). The last one is really a summary of the others. Only the first horse and its rider are controversial. Some interpreters have seen the rider as Christ, since a similar image appears in 19:11; others have seen it as a reference to the spread of the gospel. In the context of John's message both of those interpretations seem farfetched. It is obvious that this rider comes to conquer the earth with military might; that is consistent with the rest of the series. In other words, this rider represents an attempt to wield earthly power, like the "kings of the earth." The white horse is really juxtaposed to the one in 19:11, just as John contrasts Babylon and the new Jerusalem or the throne of the beast with that of God. All four of these horses and riders point to disasters that result from the misuse of human power, unlike the natural catastrophes we have examined. The result is the death of a fourth of the earth (in this case probably meaning the human population).

When the fifth seal is opened (6:9), the scene shifts abruptly from earth to heaven, where John sees the souls of those who have been martyred. It is only with the opening of the sixth seal (6:12) that we find some of the same natural calamities that we saw in the trumpet and bowl cycles. There is an earthquake; the sun and moon and stars are all affected; the sky itself rolls up like a window shade when you let it loose; and on earth the mountains and islands are obliterated. Otherwise everything else is normal! The opening of the seventh seal (8:1) produces nothing but silence in heaven, followed by an angel who offers the prayers of the saints to God. Then the cycle ends with the familiar thunder, rumbles, lightning, and an earthquake.

All in all, these three sets of visions produce quite a multimedia show. Just think what John could have produced with modern technology. However, John did not invent these images. Even if this is what he saw in his inspired state, when he put it in writing he used a tradition of symbols that was probably well known to his audience. Let us take a quick look at some of those.

JOHN'S SYMBOLIC TRADITION

We have used the term "plagues" several times in describing John's visions, since they have a lot in common with the stories associated with the exodus from Egypt. If you have time, you might want to reread Exodus 7:1–13:1. There the sequence of events is similar to but different from any we have seen in Revelation: (1) The river Nile turns to blood and all the fish die; (2) frogs cover the land; (3) gnats cover everything; (4) swarms of flies ruin the land; (5) all Egyptian livestock die; (6) boils affect humans and animals; (7) thunder and hail and fire come down from the skies; (8) locusts eat every tree and plant in the land; (9) the land is darkened for three days; (10) all the firstborn of Egypt die. How many of these can you find in Revelation? How has John changed the sequence?

There are also some interesting connections to the creation story. In commenting on the opening of the sixth seal, J. Massyngberde Ford suggests this:

> The order in which the universe is destroyed follows approximately the order of creation in Genesis: (1) the earth; (2) the sun; (3) the moon; (4) the stars; (5) the sky or firmament; (6) the mountains and islands, that

> is, the land revealed by the separation of the waters; (7)
> man, made in the image and likeness of God.[1]

The only problem with that suggestion, of course, is that people are not destroyed, according to Revelation 6:12–17; rather, they hide from the wrath of God.

Other scholars have pointed out ways in which the seven seals are similar to that section of the first three Gospels often referred to as the "Little Apocalypse" (Mark 13 and the parallels in Matthew 24 and Luke 21): wars; international conflict; famine; pestilence; persecution; earthquakes.[2]

In addition, it is possible to find allusions to nearly all of John's images somewhere in the Hebrew Bible or in the Jewish apocalyptic tradition. Most commentaries can help you find those sources if you are interested in pursuing them. That is not our purpose here, however, so let me just make one observation. John is very creative in the way he uses this material. He does not quote it directly (in sharp contrast, for example, to the scripture citations in the birth narratives in Matthew's Gospel). It is as though John had a mental reservoir of images that he drew on and, like any great writer or artist, reorganized into surprising new patterns. I can no longer find the source, but a reviewer once devastated a book by saying: "This book contains material that is both interesting and original. Unfortunately, what is interesting is not original, and what is original is not interesting." We cannot say that about John. He meets both criteria.

OTHER NATURAL CATASTROPHES
IN REVELATION

In addition to the plague cycles, two other major passages picture destruction from natural causes rather than from human-initiated conflicts such as war. We need to look briefly at them before we try to draw some conclusions.

The first passage describes the fall of Babylon (Revelation 17—18). What a surprise! John just told us the city was already destroyed by the earthquake at the end of the bowl visions (16:19). That fact challenges a strictly literal interpretation of the Bible and forces us to see that John's images are fluid. He takes the image from 16:19 and develops it in 18:1–24 through a series of dirges and laments. Notice that the final destruction has not yet taken place. John is projecting what people will say when it does actually happen. John's description is proleptic, a reading of the future as though it has already happened. For example, the laments by the kings in 18:9 and by the merchants in 18:15 are in the future tense: they "will weep" and "will stand far off." When the angel throws the millstone into the sea, it is a symbol of how sudden and devastating the collapse of Rome will be (18:21–24).

EXERCISE 15

The second passage is a short one that we have not mentioned yet. Read 14:14–20. What is going on here? Who are the characters? What images do you find?

This is one of the more difficult passages in Revelation to understand. It is clear that there are two separate images here: harvest and a winepress. In John's tradition (especially in Joel 3:13), both are images of a final judgment. In the Gospels the image of the harvest includes both the gathering of the faithful and a last judgment. However, some details remain confusing.

The first has to do with the identity of the "Son of Man" who has a golden crown and holds a sickle (14:14). The obvious choice is the risen Christ, since in John's opening vision he has already described Christ as "one like the Son of Man" (1:13). The only problem here is that in 14:15 John refers to "another angel" (one of six in the section 14:6–20), implying that Christ is on the same level. Commentators have found ingenious ways to solve this problem, but there is no question that John wants us to see that it is Jesus Christ who is about to carry out God's final judgment on humankind.

A second question is whether these are two different images of the same event, or whether the first (harvest) implies a gathering of the righteous, while the second (vintage) implies condemnation of the unrighteous. The winepress image is certainly more vivid, with blood several feet high flowing for nearly two hundred miles. My personal inclination is to see both images as duplicates of the same event; but ultimately that choice does not change our understanding of John's total message.

The third issue is that John seems to have put this passage too early in his book. If it is a picture of the final judgment, why does it come before the last set of plagues and the fall of Babylon? This is also a difficult question to answer, but several other times we think we have reached the end, only to have John move on to a new topic. For example, at the end of each plague cycle we are prepared for a description of the return of Christ. In 10:6, a voice from heaven tells John that "there will be no more delay" once the seventh trumpet has sounded, but there is a delay. When the seventh bowl is poured out a voice from the throne announces, "It is done!" but it is not done. From a literary point of view, we might suspect that John has received his visions at different times, each one preparing us for the conclusion, and has then combined them into a series.

UNDERSTANDING THE IMAGES

What we have done so far is to describe John's imagery with very few attempts to explain it. Now it is time to draw some conclusions and to deal with the meaning of his images.

1. One characteristic of apocalyptic literature is the idea that things are going to get worse before they get better. In fact, the world is so evil that God may have to destroy it. The time before the end, then, will be one of chaos and tribulation and suffering.[3] If you remember, there is a kind of progression in the amount of violence. With the opening of the fourth seal, a quarter of the earth dies (6:8). In the trumpet cycle, nearly a third of everything is destroyed. When the bowls are poured out, the death toll is not recorded except for the sea creatures, who are totally wiped out. Yet we get the impression that the suffering is fairly extensive.

2. Another basic question is, How are the three cycles (seals, trumpets, and bowls) related to one another? One answer, taking John's account literally, is that they refer to successive periods of human history. The destruction of the world will occur in a series of natural disasters, each more serious than the one before. Another answer, primarily from a literary point of view, is that they are simply different versions of the same events, which John either received or wrote down at different times. This answer applies better to the last two cycles than to the first one. A third answer is that in some sense they repeat or recapitulate each other, like a spiral, taking previous images and moving them to another level. Which view makes more sense to you? You may want to add this to the list of questions for discussion at the end of this chapter.

3. Who or what is responsible for these disasters? Clearly God, as creator, is ultimately responsible for a world where such disasters happen. The plagues are different because they are a concentrated series of events and more spectacular. They are also symbols of God's wrath—that is, God's judgment against what is evil. John uses two different Greek words for God's "wrath," one of them ten times and the other seven times. In 15:1 and 16:19 the plagues are explicitly described with those terms. In 6:16–17 the sixth plague is seen as the wrath of the one on the throne and the Lamb. Sometimes the image is one of drinking the wine of God's wrath (e.g., in 14:10 and 16:19); in contrast, Babylon "made all nations drink of the wine of the wrath of her fornication" (14:8). John has reworked images of the "day of the Lord," which in his tradition is a day of judgment. Earthquakes are a powerful force in that part of the world. In October of 1995, a quake destroyed most of the houses in a city of one hundred thousand not far from the cities to which John was writing. For him, the earthquake that closes each cycle of plagues announces God's presence as judge. In more technical language, it marks a theophany or appearance of God.[4]

4. Who actually suffers during these catastrophes? If you read carefully, you noticed in every case that the ones who suffer are those who worshiped the beast or who did not have God's seal on their foreheads.[5] They belong to the kingdom of Satan, not to the kingdom of God. The plagues are directed at the world outside the church, just as in Exodus they were directed against Pharaoh and the Egyptians. The church, on the other hand, is protected. Christ's message to the Christians at Philadelphia is that because of their faithful endurance "I will keep you from the hour of trial that is coming on the whole world to test the inhabitants of the earth" (3:10). Those words are spoken to one congregation, not to the church as a whole. Later, however, in the interval after the opening of the sixth seal, we learn that those who have God's seal on their foreheads will be protected (7:3). From John's perspective, the dualism of good and evil coincides with the dualism of the church and the world.

5. Finally, we may ask about the purpose of these disasters. Why do they occur? The answer is given in the quotation in the last paragraph: to "test the inhabitants of the earth." The plagues and other disasters are meant to be therapeutic. They are meant to lead people to acknowledge and worship God. They are not acts of

a vengeful God but are meant to provoke repentance. Over and over, John reminds us that the earth dwellers hide themselves from God (6:15–16) They refuse to repent (9:20–21; 16:9, 11). There is a kind of raw justice here. They made their decision to worship the beast; now they can either repent or take the consequences. Before we accuse God of not playing fair, of protecting and rewarding those who risk their lives for the sake of God and the Lamb, we must remember what John tells us about God's justice. Through God's actions, the martyrs are vindicated (6:10 and 16:5–7); their deaths, and the deaths of future martyrs, are not in vain. One of the refrains in the heavenly anthems is to praise God, whose ways are just and true (15:3) and true and just (19:2). Nevertheless, there is something unsettling, if not about the idea of retribution, then at least about John's image of a God who destroys Babylon in order to avenge the blood of his servants (19:2). We will have to think more about John's theology in a later chapter.

QUESTIONS FOR DISCUSSION

1. Do you think that John expected the plagues to occur exactly as he described them?

2. When do you think John expected these things to happen: in his own lifetime, in the near future, at some specific time in the distant future?

3. When John talks about all the sea creatures being destroyed, do you think that is a fate that humans could conceivably experience if they are not environmentally conscious?

4. Do you think John portrays God as a vindictive tyrant who wants to coerce people into being Christians?

CHAPTER 7

Images of Military Conflict

John had a contemporary named Epictetus. Originally a Roman slave, he gained his freedom, became a philosopher, won patronage from the emperor Domitian, and was later banished from Rome to Asia Minor. He wrote the *Enchiridion*, a classic of the Stoic philosophy, which was one of Christianity's most attractive competitors. The book was a manual of instruction for officers in the Roman army. However, its focus was not on the tactics of warfare. Instead, it spelled out the attitude or the philosophy of life that soldiers should have. It told them how to act according to natural law and maintain control of their own lives.

In one sense Revelation is like that manual. It prepares Christians to face combat, both earthly and spiritual, which may turn out to be mortal. Those in the seven churches are promised a reward if they "conquer," and they are instructed how to live in a war zone. Images of war are pervasive in Revelation, so let us look at them more closely.

WARS AND RUMORS OF WAR

EXERCISE 16
Revelation either records or anticipates a number of wars. Read 12:1–13:7; 16:14–16; 17:9–14; 19:11–20:15. Who does the fighting? Where does it occur? Who are the victims?

These are not normal battles! Two different kinds of war are pictured in these passages. The most important ones describe a heavenly warfare, and humans are not involved at all. First in this sequence is the war between Michael and Satan, each of whom has a supporting cast of angels (12:7–9). The result is that Satan (the dragon) is expelled from heaven and thrown to the earth. After this, there is no more fighting in heaven. A second battle will take place between the Lamb and the kings of the earth. In 16:14–16 we are told that this battle will occur at some mythical place called Harmagedon. The tension is heightened in 17:9–14, where we are told that the battle will include the beast and ten kings who have not yet received power. When the battle finally does take place (19:11–21), the location is not mentioned, although we can assume it is an earthly one. The beast and the false prophet (the second beast) are thrown into the lake of fire. In the next chapter we will look at this passage in more detail to see how the victory is actually won. After this comes a victory over Satan himself, occurring in two stages. He is thrown into the pit by an angel (20:1–3), then released for reasons that are not clear. Gog and Magog, representing the nations at the ends of the earth, support Satan in an attack on the faithful community (the "beloved city") but are consumed by fire from heaven. The second victory over Satan occurs as he is thrown into the lake of fire and sulfur to join the beast and the false prophet (20:7–10). Finally, Death and Hades suffer the same fate (20:14). The warfare is ended!

A second kind of warfare appears in the passages you just read. These occur on earth, and they do involve human victims. The beast from the pit makes war on the two prophets and kills them. Their bodies lie unburied for three and a half days until they are taken up into heaven (11:7–13). The dragon tries to kill the woman's son (12:4). He is unsuccessful, but later he does make war on her other children (12:17). Those who worship the beast feel that no one can fight against it (13:4). On the other hand, the beast is allowed to make war on the saints and conquer them (13:7).

In these earthly wars it is Christians (the "saints") who are the victims. If the plagues show Christians as being exempt from harm, just the opposite is true here. A government that does not want to recognize any limits on its power, and that wants undivided loyalty from its subjects, will try to eliminate those Christians who refuse its demands. Within the past three months before I wrote that sentence, Rev. Manuel Saquic, a young Presbyterian pastor in Guatemala, was assassinated for protesting human rights violations by his government. He disappeared on his way home from a meeting, and his body was later discovered in an unmarked grave. The government refused to investigate his death or to allow his family to give him a Christian burial. Other church leaders who have asked the government to find his killers and bring them to justice have received death threats. Although John knew nothing about these events, he would not have been surprised.

Revelation is really a subversive book. When I suggested at the beginning of this chapter that Revelation is a manual for Christians living in a time of war, I should have added something important. It does not tell Christians how to engage in war but rather how to resist. It is a resistance manual.

The passages you read in Exercise 16 describe two types of war—those in heaven and those against the saints. Remember, though, that some of the plagues also involve warfare. The four horsemen come to conquer and fight. The demonic armies released after the fifth and sixth trumpets attack only the enemies of God. So we have to add a third category of war: those in which God's justice is directed against the inhabitants of the earth.

THE CONDUCT OF WAR

EXERCISE 17

Read Revelation 9. Look at John's description of the troops and their equipment. What is different about them?

John gives us some vivid pictures of these mythical armies. The hybrid horses are a clear signal that these are demonic creatures, not ones you are going to see at your state fair or even at Ripley's "Believe It or Not" exhibit. In the first of these two visions, the locusts are like horses outfitted for battle, yet they have tails like scorpions. They have scales like breastplates and their wings sound like chariots (9:9). In the second vision, the riders are wearing the breastplates (9:17). The horses have heads like lions and their tails are serpents. What causes the destruction, however, is the fire and smoke and sulfur that come from the horses' mouths. The demonic aspect of this vision comes from the association of those elements with the underworld. Smoke rises from the bottomless pit when it is opened (9:2). The lake into which the beast, the false prophet, Satan, and Death and Hades are thrown is associated with sulfur (19:20; 20:10). If you have ever stared into the core of a volcano, you know exactly how this image of the underworld originated.

The rider in 6:2 carries a bow. Most commentaries will tell you that John's readers would have associated this symbol with the Parthians, traditional enemies of Rome from the land beyond the Euphrates (roughly present-day Iran), who were capable of shooting with the bow while riding horseback.

The second rider carries a sword (6:4). Actually, Revelation uses two different words for "sword." One, the "two-edged sword," is used almost exclusively for Jesus Christ; the only exception is in 6:8. We will look at those passages in the next chapter. The term used here is associated in the biblical tradition with eschatological judgment. It is used again in 13:14 for the beast who had been wounded but not killed. The most interesting use of the term is found in 13:10, taken from Jeremiah 15:2 and reinterpreted by John. It opens in 13:9 with the same formula of advice that we saw in the letters to the seven churches: "Let anyone who has an ear listen." It then tells them that if they are to be taken captive, go; the implication is "go willingly." It then tells them, "If you kill with the sword, with the sword you must be killed." Far from giving Christians permission to take up arms, it warns them not to do it. In other words, don't become like those who use force against you. One of the older commentators puts it succinctly: "The admonitory words at the beginning and the end of vv. 9–10 show that the whole passage is a warning to the readers regarding their steadfastness and the avoidance of force in resisting persecution."[1]

THE LANGUAGE OF POWER

In chapter 5 above, we looked at three dimensions of conflict in the Apocalypse: within the church, between the church and other religious claims, and between church and empire. Through the imagery of warfare we now discover that the conflict has another dimension. Behind internal conflicts that threaten the integrity of the church, behind other religions that challenge Christianity, and especially behind any government that promotes idolatry, John sees a group of demonic, mythic, transcendent powers. These include Satan and all the characters who carry out his work. The conflict has a cosmic dimension.

In addition, there is other language of power in Revelation which focuses on ruling rather than on fighting, on God as king rather than as warrior. It also has a cosmic dimension.

EXERCISE 18

Look again at the following passages: 1:4–11; chapters 4—5; 11:15–19; 15:3–4; and 19:1–8. Make a list of words or images that help you to understand the meaning of power in Revelation. The same themes appear in many other places in the book, but we will focus just on these few verses.

1. All these passages emphasize God's kingdom or rule. Without going through each passage separately, we can draw some quick conclusions. First of all, God is the source of all power. God is the "almighty" (1:8; 4:8; 11:17; 15:3; 19:6), the one worthy to receive glory and power (4:11; 19:1). God reigns (11: 17; 19:6) as the king of the nations (15:3).

Second, God now shares that rule with Jesus Christ, who is "the ruler of the kings of the earth" (1:5; 11:15; see also 12:10). The Lamb is also worthy to receive power and all the other accolades to which God is entitled (5:12).

Most surprising, perhaps, is that Christ has now shared that kingdom with his followers, making them a kingdom and priests (1:6; 5:10). Christ's rule has not yet been established on earth, as we acknowledge whenever we say the Lord's Prayer. Yet John has no doubt that Christ's faithful followers will reign with him (5:10), a promise he describes as being fulfilled in the thousand-year rule (20:4–6).

Opposed to God's rule, of course, are the kings of the earth. They prostitute themselves with the power of the great city (17:2; 18:3, 9), but eventually they will turn and destroy it (17:16). They also plot war against the Lamb, as though they were powerful enough to win. The last we hear of them is that they have become a feast for the birds of prey (19:21).

2. Another dominant image throughout Revelation is that of the throne, as we noticed when we talked about places. It is used more than sixty times in this book, three times as often as in all the rest of the New Testament. It is John's oblique way of referring to God. This image communicates a sense of God's glory. Those

who approach the throne are coming into God's presence. It also communicates a sense of God's power, although not everyone acknowledges that fact. In addition, the image communicates God's justice, as we saw especially in 19:1–5. The throne image almost always occurs in the context of worship and praise. Moreover, God has shared with Christ not just the kingdom but also the throne. Note in 7:17 that the Lamb at the center of the throne becomes their shepherd. Finally, just as Christ will share the rule with the saints, so he will share the throne with those who conquer (3:21).

There is, of course, a rival throne, that of Satan and the beast. It has the power to wage war against the saints, but John's message is simple. It cannot win.

3. One other symbol, out of many that we might choose, is the crown. It symbolizes both power and victory. Normally it is associated with triumph. For example, Christians in Smyrna who remain faithful to death are promised the crown of life, while those in Philadelphia are encouraged to hold fast to it so that no one steals it. Apparently it can be either won or lost.

In the heavenly vision scene, the twenty-four elders are wearing gold crowns (4:4), which they later toss before the throne as part of their praise and worship (4:10). In the judgment scene in which the Son of Man appears, he is also wearing a gold crown (14:14).

The mother of the male child, who appears mysteriously in Revelation 12 clothed with the sun and with the moon under her feet, is wearing a crown with twelve stars (12:1). From a purely literary viewpoint, the woman is a figure of great authority whose son is born to rule the nations (an obvious reference to 1:5) and is taken up to God's throne (another fairly obvious reference to Christ). She is then taken to the wilderness, where she is protected (12:13–16); but then the dragon pursues the rest of her children (12:17). For John's audience, the image of the crown might conjure up a whole range of associations, from the twelve tribes of Israel to the signs of the zodiac and the worship of the Mother Goddess in Asia Minor. Commentators have a field day with this passage. The simplest explanation is that the woman who gives birth represents the nation of Israel, the mother of the Messiah, who then becomes the true Israel and gives birth to "those who keep the commandments of God and hold the testimony of Jesus" (12:17).

Of course, we have come to expect that any symbol in Revelation will have its countersymbol, and that is true here as well. The first rider (6:2) is also wearing a crown, which suggests that his ability to conquer on earth is derived from God, who delegates that power through the first living creature. That word appears once more in the locust plague (9:7). It is qualified by the adverb "like," used in one form or another three times in the same verse. I remember hearing a number of years ago an Englishman complain about a bearded young man whom he met on a plane flight and asked him what he did for a living. The reply was, "Hey, like, ya know, man, I'm into teaching English." John's grammar here is not quite that bad, but he wants the reader to know that this crown is really a fake.

CONCLUSIONS

Although I have not set aside a section at the ends of most other chapters to draw conclusions, in this case it seems appropriate. Three comments are in order.

1. To understand the "cosmic powers," think of unseen forces in our own world: electricity, wind, a sexual attraction. All of these are usually helpful, but they may also become destructive: a short circuit, a tornado, a "fatal attraction." Think also of the power a demagogue has to lead a nation into war, or a financier to make millions of dollars from junk bonds that people have depended on for their retirement.

2. In terms of the war imagery, keep in mind that all the war symbols are metaphors. If there was actually a war in heaven, what qualifies John as an international observer? Are the future cosmic battles of God and the Lamb versus Satan and his forces something that you would expect to record and videotape? Or are they an imaginative way of saying that there are unseen forces in the world that are powerful, attractive, and elusive?

Similarly, the earthly battles in Revelation are real in the sense that Christians will have to suffer and perhaps even die. If Christians are to be faithful, they can expect to have to suffer. There will be conflict. However, John is not predicting a specific battle or war, not even the fall of Rome (which did occur over three hundred years later) or a war in the Persian Gulf or one in the Holy Land.

3. In Revelation, Christians are never given permission to inflict violence or to use a weapon. Then how are they to "conquer"?

Thus far we have seen that they must not compromise, they must resist, and they must remain faithful. There is more to it than that, as we will see below in chapter 15.

QUESTIONS FOR DISCUSSION

1. Do you think Christians should obey the state because it has been ordained by God, or do you think they may resist if the state seems to be corrupt? What about other institutions that demand our total loyalty?

2. Do you agree that Revelation is a kind of "resistance manual"? If so, does it tell you when and how to resist?

3. If the choice were up to you, would you include Revelation in the Bible? Why or why not?

CHAPTER 8

The Cosmic Victor

Another man who was writing a book about the Apocalypse was really proud of himself for having unlocked the book's secrets. In fact, he was so proud of himself that he bragged about it to his New York City cab driver. Then he made the mistake of asking the cabbie whether he understood the book's message. "Of course I do" came the reply. "Well, then, what is it?" the author asked. His answer was this: "God wins." He was right, although perhaps he should have said, "God and the Lamb win."

THE DECISIVE BATTLE

EXERCISE 19

The key battle is the one between the Lamb and the kings of the earth in 19:11–21. You have read it before, but read it one more time. Who wins? How? Make a list of the symbols in this passage and try to remember where in Revelation you saw them before.

This is John's vision of the return of Christ, the Parousia. It is the event we have been waiting for since 1:7: "Look! He is coming with the clouds; every eye will see him, even those who pierced him; and on his account all the tribes of the earth will wail." It is the event we should have expected at the end of each plague cycle, and we were also prepared for it in 17:14. At the same time, it marks a transition to the final events in history: the defeat of Satan (twice), the resurrection of the faithful martyrs to rule with Christ for a thousand years, a second general resurrection, the defeat of Death and Hades, and the appearance of the new heaven and earth and the holy city. Thus the passage plays a key role in the entire Apocalypse.

Some literary features of this passage we should note before we look at it in detail. First, we know that something dramatic is about to happen when John begins by saying, "Then I saw heaven opened" (19:11). The only other time John used that phrase was when he announced the first throne vision (4:1), where only a door into heaven was open. Second, John's style adds to the excitement and drama, since he uses the word "and" thirty-one times in these eleven verses; the English translations tend to smooth out the style. Third, some commentators take the phrase "Then I saw" (literally "And I saw") as a key to the structure of the section beginning in 19:11. They find a set of seven visions, dividing our passage at 19:17. That argument is not convincing. For one thing, you can see even in an English translation that John uses the phrase "and I saw" more than seven times: in 19:11, 17, 19; 20:1, 4 (twice), 11, 12; 21:1; and in a slightly different grammatical sequence in 21:2, 22. He does not use the phrase in connection with the defeat of Satan (20:7–10), which is almost certainly another vision. Instead, John presents the entire section 19:11–21 as a single unit. The rider on the white horse frames the whole section, in the opening and closing verses. The sword mentioned in 19:15 is mentioned again in 19:21, tying those sections together. The rider in 19:11 "makes war," just as the kings of the earth do in 19:19; and the armies of heaven (19:14) are counterbalanced by the armies of the beast and the kings of the earth (19:19). It is a wonderfully constructed unit.

Who wins the battle? Without a doubt it is the rider on the white horse. But who is he? John gives us all kinds of clues. First, the rider has a number of names: "faithful and true" (19:11), one known only to himself (19:12), the "Word of God" (19:13),[1] and "King of kings and Lord of lords" (19:16). That last verse is the clincher. It refers back to 17:14, where the titles are used in the opposite sequence and the figure is identified as the Lamb. Also, 1:5 introduces Jesus Christ as "the faithful witness," and the letter to Laodicea is from the one who is "the faithful and true witness" (3:14). As alert readers, you now know who the rider is.

In addition to the names, how many symbols did you find in this passage? It is loaded with them, nearly twenty-five by my count. We can look at only a few of them, just to see how John picks up clues that he dropped early in the book. For example, the "eyes like a flame of fire" (19:12) recalls the opening vision (1:14) and the letter to Thyatira (2:18). The double-edged sword was also mentioned in the opening vision (1:16) and twice in the letter to Pergamum (2:12, 16, where Christ threatens to come and make war against them). It is also mentioned twice here (19:15, 21). The robe dipped in blood apparently refers to his own death. All these symbols reinforce the identity of the rider on the white horse. The winepress is a reminder of the deadly judgment scene in 14:17–20 and other passages that spoke of drinking the wine cup of God's wrath. By now you recognize the mark of the beast (19:20) as a familiar symbol of idolatry.

What does the rider (the Lamb) do? Two very important things. He "judges and makes war" (19:11). John has transferred to Christ two of the most important images of God in the Hebrew Bible, those of judge and warrior. The two images are intertwined in Revelation but nowhere more closely than in this passage. Christ's return marks the beginning of the final judgment, which involves the defeat of the forces of evil (both earthly and demonic), the resurrection of the faithful, and then a resurrection of all others to be judged according to their works.[2] As a warrior, Christ defeats the armies of the kings of the earth, bringing to an end—except for the strange reprieve in 20:7–10—human rebellion against God.

How does he do it? This is perhaps the strangest part of all. Today movies and TV shows tend to focus on the battles and fight scenes, including all kinds of gratuitous violence. John, on the other hand, never does describe the battle. All he tells us is that "the rest were killed by the sword of the rider on the horse, the sword that came from his mouth" (19:21). Is this simply John's way of saying that "the pen is mightier than the sword"? No, it goes deeper than that. The sword is the word of God, the "testimony of Jesus Christ" that was announced at the very beginning of the book (1:2). The victory is won not in a military bloodbath but metaphorically by the power of the gospel.

THE LAMB AS VICTIM AND VICTOR

EXERCISE 20

If you have been doing all the exercises, you are probably tired of reading Revelation. Nevertheless, read it one more time to see what you can learn about the Lamb. How is he described? What does he do?

The first time we meet the Lamb, of course, is in Revelation 5, as part of the heavenly vision. The scene is set when John describes his despair because no one has been found capable of opening the seven seals. One of the twenty-four elders announces that "the Lion of the tribe of Judah, the Root of David, has conquered" and can open the seals (5:5). This is messianic language. It identifies Jesus as the descendant of David, the greatest king of Israel who came from Judah, the most southern of the twelve tribes of Israel. The lion is a symbol of power and authority, so as John turns, we expect him to meet a creature of overwhelming greatness. Instead, John sees "a Lamb standing as if it had been slaughtered" (5:6), a shocking reversal of images. This Lamb seems to be a symbol of weakness and failure, not one of power. Yet as we keep reading we have another surprise, because the Lamb has seven horns and seven eyes (5:6). Seven is the number for completeness or perfection. Thus the seven horns symbolize total power (omnipotence) and the seven eyes symbolize total knowledge (omniscience). The slaughtered Lamb is, after all, the most powerful of all creatures, sharing the attributes of God! This may be the best example in Revelation of the way in which John transforms an image so that it has multiple meanings. Just when we think we have grasped it, he adds another nuance. The image is not just ambivalent, having two meanings; it is multivalent, having several meanings at the same time.

Throughout the rest of the book the Lamb reveals this multivalent character. Earlier in the book, Christ was introduced as "the firstborn of the dead, and the ruler of the kings of the earth" (1:5). In John's first vision, Christ tells him, "I was dead, and see, I am alive forever and ever" (1:18). The Lamb is praised by creatures in heaven and on earth because he was slaughtered; yet he deserves the same kind of worship to which God is entitled (5:9–14). He is the one who opens the seven seals (6:1–8:1). He appears on Mount Zion along with the 144,000 who have been redeemed (14:1–5), a sign of their victory. One of the beatitudes blesses those invited to the marriage supper of the Lamb (19:9). When the heavenly city appears, God and the Lamb take the place of the temple (21:22). The Lamb is a victorious figure, just as he is in the final battle scene. But how is his victory accomplished?

The key is found in Revelation 12:7–12. At first glance, it is Michael and his angels who defeat the dragon. Then a loud voice from heaven interprets the victory: "But they have conquered him [Satan] by the blood of the Lamb and by the word of their testimony" (12:11). It was the Cross and resurrection that conquered Satan. Christ's defeat was transformed into victory, his death into eternal life. The pattern was set for those who want to be faithful to him, "for they did not cling to life even in the face of death" (12:11).

This Lamb who was slain is the same one who is the ruler of the kings of the earth, who shares the throne with God the Almighty, and who shares both the throne and the kingdom with his loyal followers. The victim is the victor. The Lamb wins! Christ is victorious!

QUESTIONS FOR DISCUSSION

1. Even though John does not describe an actual battle in 19:11–21, a lot of carnage is depicted at the end. The flesh of Christ's enemies is being picked over by the birds like so much roadkill. Do you think John meant this literally—that is, that non-Christians will eventually die in some kind of holocaust?

2. From your own study, what else can you say about John's portrait of the Lamb? Do you think he makes a convincing case that the way to victory is through the Cross?

3. In a nonagricultural society, very few of us have had any experience with lambs. If you were writing a book such as Revelation today, what image would you use to make the point that victory often comes as a result of suffering?

PART THREE

John's Images in Context

The New Testament Context

Some of John's ideas—or at least his way of expressing them—seem to be original, such as his picture of the Lamb. No matter what he actually saw in his visions, however, his written descriptions use a lot of images that are found in other apocalyptic writings and in the Hebrew Bible. In part 3, we will look at selected passages that contain similar ideas. John may have known them, but he does not quote them as "sources," as if he were writing a term paper today. Some passages may have been part of the early Christian preaching; others belonged to his Jewish heritage.

To keep our task manageable the focus will be on images of a final conflict and of a cosmic victor. By discovering where those images came from and how they developed, we can better appreciate John's use of them. In chapter 9 we will focus on three New Testament passages.

CHRIST AND THE RESURRECTION

EXERCISE 21
Read 1 Corinthians 15:20–28, especially verses 23–28. What stages does Paul include in his picture of the final (eschatological) events? What does he mean by being "subject"?

First Corinthians 15:20–28 is part of the famous chapter in which Paul discusses the resurrection. First Corinthians 16:8 indicates that the letter was written from Ephesus, during Paul's stay of three or more years there, as reported in Acts 19. It is the oldest of the three passages we will study in this chapter. It undoubtedly reflects ideas that Paul and his associates used during their preaching missions in Asia Minor, in the same area to which Revelation was addressed.

All of 1 Corinthians 15 rests on a formula found in 15:3–5, which is the earliest Christian statement about the resurrection. Paul had *reported* it to the Corinthians as something he had *received* (15:3), both terms for the passing on of a tradition; and he reminds them that Jesus' resurrection was an essential part of his preaching when he was with them in Corinth (15:1–2). In the rest of the chapter, Paul builds on this core of his preaching to answer certain questions, or to correct some misunderstandings, that the Corinthians had about the resurrection of believers. In fact, it appears that some Christians there believed they had already been raised with Christ. That gave them special wisdom (1:18–3:23) and special knowledge (8:1), made them kings (4:8), and made it lawful to do whatever they wanted (6:12; 10:23). In contrast, Paul insists that the resurrection of believers is still in the future, not something they have already experienced.

In the passage you have read, we met two ideas not found in Revelation. One is the "first fruits" (15:20, 23), a metaphor of the beginning of a harvest. It is a sign that Christ's resurrection is the beginning of a new creation. The other one contrasts Adam and Christ, depicting them as ideal types (15:21–22; cf. Romans 5:12–21). Adam represents humanity in rebellion against God and therefore subject to sin and ultimately to death. Christ represents a new humanity liberated from the law, sin, and death. Both ideas are important for Paul's thought, but they do not need to concern us here.

The section closest to Revelation is found in 15:23–26. Paul pictures a sequence of events. First, God has already raised Christ from the dead. Next, Christ will come in the near future and "those who belong" to him will be raised (15:23). He will rule until he has "destroyed every ruler and every authority and power" (15:24), that is, "put all his enemies under his feet" (15:25, 27). Earlier in the letter Paul reminded them, "Do you not know that the saints will judge the world?" (6:2). He does not say that again here, but apparently he assumes that the saints who have been raised will rule with him. Once the victory has been won, including the defeat of death itself (15:26), Christ will turn the kingdom over to God, who remains the supreme authority (15:24, 27–28).

What in this scene agrees with the imagery of Revelation? First, Christ is the cosmic victor, the one who will eventually defeat all the powers of evil and establish God's kingdom. Second, there is a definite sequence of events that both writers expect to take place in the future, in roughly the same order. Finally, even death is abolished; it is the last victim.

On the other hand, there are some important differences. For one thing, Paul does not describe a war; the battle imagery may be implicit but it is subdued. Second, Christ's reign has no definite time period, such as the thousand-year rule (millennium) that we found in Revelation. Third, Paul does not state that this world will be destroyed and replaced by a new heaven and a new earth. His vision is closer to that of the earlier biblical prophets who expected God's rule to be established on this earth as a result of a radical reformation. The fourth and most significant difference is that Paul expects Christ to remain subordinate to God the Father. Given his strong background in Jewish monotheism, Paul cannot quite bring himself to assert the equality of God and Christ in the way that we have seen in Revelation. In Paul's letter they do not share the throne or the kingdom; God remains "all in all" (15:28). In this sense, Revelation has a "higher" Christology, or view of Christ, one closer to that of the Fourth Gospel than to Paul.

CHRIST THE FIRSTBORN

EXERCISE 22

Now read Colossians 1:15–20; 2:8–15; and 3:1–4. Do you notice any differences from the passage we just examined in 1 Corinthians 15? If so, how would you explain them? What issue or issues seem to be the main concern in these passages?

If you check the map on page vi of this book, you will see that Colossae was located about eighty miles east of Ephesus, not far from the territory to which John's seven letters were sent. The opening and closing verses of Colossians suggest that it was written by Paul to a church he had never visited. However, many contemporary scholars believe that the letter was not actually written by Paul but by one of his close associates after Paul's death. Arguments based on vocabulary and style are not really decisive. Neither is the historical setting, although the issues raised in the

letter sound more like the Gnostic controversies of the second
century than first-generation Christianity. More compelling are
the different *ideas*. One has to do with warnings against a strange
philosophy (in the section beginning with 2:8) and strange rituals
(2:16–19). Second, while Paul often spoke of the church as the
body of Christ, here the metaphor refers to Christ as the head of
the body, the church (1:18, 24; 2:19). A third difference is found
in the statement that believers have already been raised with
Christ (2:12; 3:1). As we already saw in 1 Corinthians 15, Paul em-
phatically rejected that idea. If Paul did write Colossians, then his
view of the resurrection has shifted dramatically. Otherwise, these
verses give us insight into the situation in Asia Minor in the years
after Paul's death.

The passage in 1:15–20 has generated a whole body of interpretation. Most scholars now treat the passage as an early Christian hymn or confession. The literary structure is clearer when it
is printed in a poetic form, but we can easily see that the statement
"the firstborn of all creation" in the first stanza (1:15) is balanced
by "the beginning, the firstborn from the dead" (in the middle of
1:18), probably marking a new stanza. The entire passage celebrates the cosmic victor, as do the hymns in Revelation 5. In
Christ the fullness of God's power was present (1:19). He existed
before creation (1:15, 17). Not only is Christ the one through
whom all powers were created (1:15); he is the one in whom all
conflicts will eventually be resolved (1:20).

What are some differences between this Colossians passage and
Revelation? One is the emphasis on the fact that Christ is the
"firstborn of all creation," the one through whom all the powers
came into being. This indeed sounds like ideas that flourished in
the next century, when Gnostic Christians believed that there
were multiple tiers or heavens in the universe, each with its own
ruler or demigod. A term used in this philosophy is *stoicheia* (2:8,
20), translated as "the elemental spirits of the universe." Although
the term can simply mean "elements" in the sense of the building
blocks of the natural world, here it seems to refer to unseen heavenly powers that had the ability to control one's destiny.[1] Colos-
sian Christians were apparently tempted to worship those powers.
The letter warns against such worship, arguing that Christ is not
just "the head of every ruler and authority" (2:10); he actually created them, whether "thrones or dominions or rulers or powers"
(1:16). A second difference is the absence of warfare imagery. The

closest analogy is the statement that Christ "disarmed" the rulers
and authorities (2:10), although that verb may imply public expo-
sure (like "the emperor who had no clothes") rather than a military image.

What is similar to the ideas we have seen in Revelation? Most
obvious is the image of Christ as the one who controls all forces,
whether legitimate or demonic. He is the cosmic victor and ruler.
Second, the kingdom image is present, although in Colossians it
is God who has "rescued us from the power of darkness and transferred us into the kingdom of his beloved Son" (1:13). Third, as in
Revelation the real victory was won on the Cross. The hymn talks
about the reconciliation of all things "through the blood of his
cross" (1:20). Also, the Cross is the place where Christ made a
public spectacle of the rulers and authorities (2:15). Although
stated differently, this language is consistent with the role of the
Cross in Revelation.

THE POWER OF CHRIST

EXERCISE 23
Finally, read Ephesians 1:15–23 and 6:10–17. Do you find anything new here? Are any familiar images used in different ways?

In part 2, I mentioned four criteria commonly used to test the
authenticity of any text. Using each of them, Ephesians turns out
to be quite different from the main body of Paul's letters. *Vocabulary:* Typical Pauline words are missing or used with new meanings; many of the new words are unique in the New Testament.
Style: Sentences are long and complicated (1:3–14 and 1:15–23
are each one sentence in the Greek text). *Historical setting:* The
critical issue of Paul's time—whether or not to admit Gentiles
into the church—has long been resolved (2:11–22); instead, the
concern here is the future of the church as an institution, an issue
that reflects the situation at the end of the first century. *Ideas:*
Typical Pauline ideas are missing, such as the coming of Christ;
new ones appear, such as the mystery of God's plan of salvation
(1:3–14), Christ's descent into hell (4:9), and the church as the
bride of Christ (5:24–33). These issues are explained in every

major commentary, so you can look there for more details. In addition, it looks as though Ephesians borrowed from Colossians because there are so many parallels between the two letters. Finally, the title and the words "in Ephesus" (1:1) are missing from the very earliest manuscripts. The most logical conclusion to all this evidence is that Ephesians was a general letter, written to a number of churches in Asia Minor (as was Revelation), at least a generation after Paul. Paul is presented as a heroic figure, an interpreter of God's mysteries (3:1–6; 6:19–20). Ephesians adapts Paul's theology to a new situation; it is a great tribute to him.

Ephesians is more preoccupied with the cosmic aspects of power than is any other New Testament writing.[2] The language reflects a different view of the universe. For example, in the first passage you find a whole series of what we would consider synonyms: power/energy/might/strength (1:19), which God put to work or energized in Christ (1:20). This is followed by a series of agencies through which power was delivered: rule/authority/power/dominion/names. In the second Christian century, this way of thinking became familiar. The whole universe was thought to be populated with various powers: some benevolent, some demonic, some magical. Each controlled a different space, such as "the ruler of the power of the air" (2:2) and "the rulers and authorities in the heavenly places" (3:10). Christians must struggle not with the state but "against the rulers, against the authorities, against the cosmic powers of this present darkness, against the spiritual forces of evil in the heavenly places" (6:12). In addition, Ephesians maintains a temporal distinction between "this age and the age to come" (1:21).

Christ is presented as the one who rules over all these powers, not because he created them (as in Colossians), but because of the resurrection. God "raised him from the dead and seated him at his right hand" (1:20). God's right hand is a symbol of absolute authority and power, a phrase drawn from Psalm 110:1. Using spatial imagery, Ephesians declares that Christ is "far above" all these powers (1:21) and has "put all things under his feet" (also drawn from Psalm 110). Similarly, 4:8 reflects on Christ's ascension.

Ephesians has developed one aspect of the cosmic victor image, that of the struggle against unseen spiritual forces. They are no longer represented in the graphic visual forms that we saw in Revelation. Instead, it is a more conceptual, or philosophical, way of viewing the universe.

Differences from Revelation are rather striking. For one thing, John's eschatology has disappeared. No longer is there an emphasis on the fact that Christ is coming soon. In fact, there is no mention at all of his coming again! Instead, believers have already been raised with Christ and are seated with him in the heavenly places; their salvation is assured (2:4–10). The one reference to "the kingdom of Christ and of God" (5:5) suggests that the kingdom is already present in the church and that immoral persons are to be excluded. Second, Christ's victory is no longer linked to the Cross. The Cross is still important as a means by which God has reconciled Jew and Gentile to God and to each other in the body of Christ (2:16); but Christ's victory was won in the resurrection and ascension. Finally, the warfare imagery is present in a very dramatic form in 6:10–17. Ephesians describes how each article of armor will enable Christians to fight against "the wiles of the devil" (6:11) and all other spiritual enemies. But notice what has happened. It is no longer Christ who fights the battle; it is the church. The struggle is no longer a religious one or a sociopolitical one but strictly a spiritual one. John's imagery of warfare has been translated into an ecclesiastical concept.

The three passages we have studied in this chapter represent a kind of trajectory within the Pauline tradition, from Paul's apocalyptic scheme through Colossians to the speculative cosmic vision of Ephesians. Revelation does not fit neatly within this progression. Just as movie theaters preview coming attractions, so John's preview has a lot in common with 1 Corinthians 15, but it represents a tradition associated more with the Gospel and letters of John. Nowhere but in Revelation do we find the image of the cosmic victor identified with the Lamb who was slain. That remains his major contribution to the use of this image within the New Testament.

QUESTIONS FOR DISCUSSION

1. If you had to teach one of the three exercises in this chapter to a junior high Sunday school class, which one would you choose? Why?

2. If you were writing a letter such as Ephesians to churches in your area, are there any unseen powers

(e.g., psychological, spiritual, physical) you might mention? If so, make a list of them. Discuss your list with the others in your group.

3. The armor described in Ephesians 6:13–17 is obsolete today. What would be a modern equivalent? Do you think an image such as this or a hymn such as "Onward, Christian Soldiers" is an appropriate metaphor for Christians to use?

CHAPTER 10

The Jewish
Apocalyptic Context

In this chapter we will take a detour outside biblical literature. Revelation was not written in a vacuum. It reflects ideas that were very much alive in John's time, particularly among dissident groups. We will look at a few typical passages, and we will focus on images that help us to understand the role of the cosmic victor. There are no exercises, but I will suggest some resources for you to use.

QUMRAN:
THE VISION OF A COSMIC WAR

In 1947, in a cave overlooking the Dead Sea, an Arab shepherd boy discovered some jars containing ancient manuscripts. Ever since news of the discovery became public, scholars and lay people have been fascinated by what the documents can tell us about ancient Judaism and the beginnings of Christianity. Perhaps you were fortunate enough to see the exhibit of the scrolls at the Library of Congress in 1993.

The discovery of the ruins of an ancient monastic community, known as Qumran, helped to identify the people who had copied/ composed/preserved the scrolls. Most evidence suggests that the inhabitants belonged to a Jewish sect called Essenes, who occupied it from the middle of the second century B.C.E. until it was abandoned about 68 C.E. Apparently the scrolls were hidden to protect them from Roman troops advancing to attack Jerusalem during the Jewish War of 66–70 C.E. Since their discovery, the scrolls have provoked controversy over a variety of issues: their ownership and where to house them; control of their publication, including a delay of more than forty years before many of them were made public; the character of the Qumran community; the significance of the scrolls. If you want to learn more about them, several excellent introductions are available.[1]

Our interest is in the scroll known initially by a title drawn from its opening sentence: "The War of the Sons of Light with the Sons of Darkness," later shortened to "The War Scroll." Its technical designation is 1QM (1 = Cave 1; Q = Qumran; M = the first letter of the Hebrew word for "war").[2] In comparison to Revelation, the differences outweigh the similarities.

First, a large portion of the scroll is a war manual.[3] Unlike Epictetus (see chapter 7 above) and unlike Revelation, the War Scroll gives an extended description of the preparation for, the conduct of, and the sequel to a series of battles. The wars will take place over a period of forty years, although every seventh year will be one of rest, so the actual fighting takes only thirty-five years. The first stage, waged against the neighboring nations who were Israel's traditional enemies and against the Kittim from Assyria and in Egypt, will occupy nine of those years. The identity of the "Kittim" has caused a lot of controversy, but the most convincing interpretation is that it refers to Rome (like John's use of the term "Babylon"). The remaining years will be spent fighting the "kings from the north." A large portion of the scroll describes the ranks in the fighting forces, based on the traditional twelve tribes of Israel, along with the inscriptions that are to be carried on the trumpets and the standards. Qualifications for participants in the army are spelled out. Age limitations exist at both ends of the scale, and persons with physical handicaps or impurities are excluded. Soldiers who have wet dreams may not fight until they have been purified. Women and children may not visit the campsites while the battle is being waged. All these restrictions sound very much like purity regulations in the Hebrew Bible. That suspicion is reinforced when we read that the priests are in charge of the combat. To mark changes in battle strategy or alignments, they blow the trumpets in distinctive ways. Some of the most moving passages are the prayers that are to be offered at crucial steps in the battle (before, during, and after). The description of the conduct of war is so complete that Yigael Yadin commented, "For the first time we find comprehensive data on military regulations in the Jewish armies during the late period of the Second Temple, containing military technical terms hitherto unknown."[4] This aspect of the scroll as a technical war manual, then, has no parallel in Revelation. The closest analogy we have seen is in Ephesians, but there it describes a strictly spiritual warfare by the Christian community.

Second, as in Revelation, this is an eschatological battle, one to be fought in the future. However, it will be fought at two levels. On earth, the righteous oppose their enemies. At the same time, at a cosmic level, the angel Michael and the heavenly army are fighting against Belial (a term for Satan found in the Old Testament) and his army. For a long time the outcome is in doubt. Michael and Belial and their forces alternate victories. In the seventh and final battle, evil is defeated once and for all. Light conquers darkness. Michael and Israel have won the right to rule over all the earth.

Third, it appears from this description that the people of the community expect to fight. The question is how literally to take the battle imagery. In the case of Revelation, I suggested that the battle was a metaphor, since no combat was actually described. Christians were being prepared to suffer and to resist but not to fight. In this case, the technical details point toward a real war to break out at some time in the future. However, the cosmic dimension points toward a more symbolic interpretation. John Collins has put it succinctly:

> It is apparent that the imagery of cosmic warfare supported a pacifist stance for most of the community's history. If indeed the members abandoned this stance in 66–68 C.E., in the belief that the Day of Vengeance had come, their fate must serve as another reminder of the harsh difference between apocalyptic imagery and military power.[5]

Fourth, this scroll has no explicit mention of a Messiah. Several of the Qumran texts refer to one or even two messiahs: one of Aaron (the priesthood) and one of Israel (a political or community leader). We cannot get into the long debate over these texts. Since they date from different time periods, it is hard to tell whether the Qumran community had a unified view of their messiah, any more than the early Christians did. However, none of the scrolls suggest that the messiah would be more than a human figure, certainly not a cosmic victor.

Finally, the decisive final victory over evil is won by God alone. Michael and the heavenly army take part, but there is no single agent corresponding to the Lamb in the Apocalypse. As the War Scroll says, God is the "man of war" and of glory, who wins the battle just as God did at the Red Sea (columns 10–11, 18). God alone is the real cosmic victor.

OTHER JEWISH APOCALYPTIC VISIONS
OF FINAL VICTORY

A whole body of Jewish literature is usually called "apocalyptic," although many modern scholars now use that term for the literary genre, as distinct from its social function ("apocalypticism") and its set of ideas about the course and end of world history ("apocalyptic eschatology").[6] Most of the works were written between 200 B.C.E and the end of the second century C.E., thus creating one of the important Jewish contexts in which Christianity developed. Copies of many of these books were found at Qumran, showing that they were much more popular in the first century than scholars had previously known. Some of these writings are included in the Apocrypha, those "hidden" books which are included as part of the canon by Roman Catholics but not by Protestants. Others are known as "Pseude-pigrapha" (writings under someone else's name) because they were attributed to famous figures of the biblical past such as Abraham or Baruch or Enoch. Christianity also produced a number of similar writings that never gained wide enough acceptance to be included in the New Testament. Most of this literature deals with the question why God permits good people to suffer—in technical terms the question of "theodicy." Almost all the texts answer the question by appealing to God's eschatological judgment. At that time, God will reward the faithful and punish sinners.

We will look at only three examples of this literature: 1 Enoch 37—71; 4 Ezra; and 2 Baruch. If you want to read them for yourself, there are several collections.[7] If your Bible includes the Apocrypha, you can also find 4 Ezra in chapters 3—14 of 2 Esdras.

First Enoch is a composite of five books from different times and settings. All of them are attributed to Enoch, seventh in the line of descent from Adam and Eve, and the only person other than Elijah who was said to have been taken into heaven without dy-ing first (Genesis 5:24). The only complete manuscripts are in Ethiopic, although the Qumran documents include portions of each book except the chapters we will examine (the "Similitudes" or "Parables"). In spite of that absence, it seems likely that the Similitudes were composed during the first century C.E., about the same time that Christianity was emerging. They consist of an introduction, three parables (chapters 38—44; 45—57; 58—69) and two conclusions, at least one of which was probably added later. Several passages seem to be spoken by Noah rather than Enoch.

As in Revelation, Enoch has a vision of the heavenly throne, surrounded by the spirits of the righteous and four archangels (chapters 39—40). There are numerous hymns of praise to the Lord of the Spirits and his Chosen One. Unlike John, Enoch goes on a heavenly journey and learns the secrets of the heavenly bodies.

The central figure in all three visions or parables is the Chosen One = the Son of Man = the Messiah. The designation "Son of Man" was first used in Daniel 7, as we shall see. Jesus frequently used it, and John's first vision identifies the risen Christ as "one like the Son of Man" (Rev. 1:13). In 1 Enoch, it clearly refers to a cosmic figure, not to a human being. He existed before creation (as in Colossians) but was hidden until he was finally revealed to the righteous (48:2–7; 62:7–8). He will sit on God's throne (e.g., 45:3; 51:3; 55:4) and carry out God's judgment with all wisdom (49:2–4). He will reward those who have remained righteous and will dwell with them on a transformed earth (48:3–6; 61:8–13). On the other hand, the day of judgment will cause great distress for sinners (e.g., 45:2; 48:8; 69:27–29). The Chosen One will destroy the kings of the earth and the powerful (46:4–7), with the help of those who are righteous (38:5–6; 48:8–9). The kings will be thrown into a deep pit = Sheol (53:1–5; 56:8) and be burned with fire (48:9; 54:1–6; 63:10). Evil, particularly in the form of those who are powerful and who reject God, will finally be defeated, even though neither book actually describes the final battle. In one passage the Chosen One/Son of Man slays all the sinners and lawless persons with the word of his mouth (62:2; cf. Rev. 19:15, 21). Thus the Son of Man in 1 Enoch, like the Lamb in John's visions, is a cosmic victor who shares God's throne and carries out God's judgment. The last chapter of the Similitudes identifies Enoch as the Son of Man (71:14). Nothing in the parables prepares us for this conclusion. It may have been added specifically to counter the Christian identification of the risen Christ as the Son of Man, the cosmic victor.

Fourth Ezra is a series of seven visions, most of which are interpreted by the angel Uriel. The opening verse makes it clear that the author is wrestling with the destruction of Jerusalem and the loss of the temple, described in poignant detail in 10:21–24. The ostensible author is Ezra, the scribe who returned from the Babylonian exile to establish the law as the basis of Israel's religion sometime around the year 400 B.C.E. (reported in Ezra and Nehemiah, especially Nehemiah 8—10). However, the figure of the eagle with twelve wings and three heads who rules the earth is a clear reference to Rome, so that this book was written after the Jewish War of 66–70 C.E. The reference to Daniel in 12:1 also confirms a later date. Ezra is told by God to write what he has seen (14:23–26), which he does by taking five scribes and dictating ninety-four books in forty days, only twenty-four of which become public (14:37–48). An interesting counterpart to John's vision of the whore Babylon is Ezra's vision of a woman grieving for her lost son (9:38ff.), who turns out to be the city of Zion (10:27, 44). As in Revelation, there are references to the drying up of the Euphrates (13:44, 47).

Ezra is preoccupied with the coming of the end. It is approaching quickly (4:26; 5:51–55), and as it does, the world becomes more and more corrupt (5:2; 14:16–17). A number of extraordinary signs will mark the period of woes before the end (5:1–13; 6:17–24; 9:1–13). The sequence of events will include the appearance of the Messiah, who will be present with the faithful for four hundred years. Then they will all die, but all of the dead will be raised and their eternal fate will be determined at the final judgment (7:28–35). In an older manuscript of Ezra, there follows a long section speculating on life after death.

Hope for the future lies with the Messiah, who is God's Son (4 Ezra 7:28; 13:37, 52). He has been hidden but will be revealed at the end of days (12:32; 13:26, 32). In one vision, he is pictured as a lion (11:37) who promises the destruction of the eagle = Rome (11:38–46). In another he will appear "like the figure of a man come up from out of the heart of the sea" who "flew with the clouds of heaven" (13:3, RSV), an early version of Superman but a positive contrast to the beast from the sea in Revelation (13:25–26). At his day (13:52), he will deliver God's people (13:26, 29) and those who have come to fight against him (13:25–38). In a variation of the victories that we have seen earlier, he will defeat his enemies not with the sword but by frying them with a stream of fire and a storm of sparks from his mouth (13:10–11), which are given a psychological interpretation: their own evil thoughts and the law will conquer them (13:37–38). Once again, then, we are confronted with the vision of a cosmic victor who is both a warrior and a judge; but in this case the warrior image predominates.

Like 4 Ezra, 2 Baruch is associated with the destruction of Jerusalem (e.g., 1:4; 3:4; 4:1; and laments in chapters 10—13; 35) and of the temple (32:2–3; 80:1–7). Written in the name of Baruch, the scribe who copied the words of the prophet Jeremiah (Jeremiah 36; 45), the fictional setting is the destruction by the Babylonians in the sixth century B.C.E. Once again, however, the real situation is the fall of Jerusalem to the Romans; the book can be dated toward the end of the first Christian century. The author receives visions in an ecstatic state, and he writes a letter to those who question God's justice (chapters 77—87). As in Revelation, there are many prayers throughout the book.

The author expects the end to come quickly (19:5; 20:1–2; 88:1–3). It will be preceded by a number of signs (25:1–4) and by a series of twelve natural disasters (27:1–15). All people on earth will experience it, although the faithful will be protected (29:1–2).

More than any of the other Jewish writings we have examined, 2 Baruch emphasizes obedience to the law and the covenant as the basis for God's judgment (e.g., 15:5; 19:1–4; 32:11; 44:7, 14; 46:5; 48:22; 51:7; 77:3; 84:5, 8). God has reserved a place for a fixed number (e.g., 21:12; 23:4–5), whose names are written in the books to be opened at the time of judgment (24:1).

The Messiah has an instrumental place in the vision of the future. He is known as God's servant and as the deliverer (70:9). Although he was hidden, he will appear at the end of the period of tribulation (29:3). A time of great prosperity and abundance will follow, in which the monsters from the sea and the earth will be food for survivors (29:4–8; cf. chapters 48—52). Eventually the Messiah will return to heaven, an event that triggers the final judgment (30:1–4). When that happens, the souls of the faithful will be saved and the Messiah's kingdom will appear (39:7; 40:3). They will experience a new paradise during the Messiah's first appearance (25:5–8) and after their resurrection (51:1–16; 73:1–74:3). A new sanctuary that has been prepared in heaven will appear (4:1–6), although the author also believes that the vessels from the earlier temple have been preserved in heaven (6:5–9). On the other hand, sinners will die by the sword at the final judgment (40:1–2; 72:2–6). Those who escape will die as a result of earthquakes or fire (70:7–10). Once again we encounter the figure of a cosmic Messiah, whose function is to reward the faithful and to destroy evil forever. He is a cosmic victor, but one whose identity is unknown until he is revealed during the last times.

It is easy to see that there are many parallels between these documents and Revelation. Even though Revelation is part of the Bible, and although John was an inspired writer, he was also part of an apocalyptic tradition that provided him with many of his images. What was unique was the way John used and transformed those images.

QUESTIONS FOR DISCUSSION

1. As you were reading this chapter, what surprised you? Make a list of things that impresssed you the most.

2. Based on what you know about Qumran, does that community sound more like the Branch Davidians (who armed themselves against attack from the outside world) or the old-order Amish (who want to live peacefully without intrusion from the outside world)? How could you give a convincing answer to that question?

3. After reading at least a summary of the Jewish apocalyptic writings, do you think John was: (*a*) a slavish imitator; (*b*) a second-rate hack; (*c*) a brilliant innovator; or (*d*) none of the above? Defend your answer.

CHAPTER 11

The Old Testament Context

In the last chapter, we looked at several Jewish apocalyptic writings. Were they a totally new kind of literature when they first appeared, or did they have roots in the Hebrew Bible? In other words, are there passages like them in the Old Testament? The answer is "Yes, but not many." Apocalyptic writers tended to be pessimistic about this world. They saw God's victory as a cosmic act that would end history and usher in a new age, in contrast to earlier prophets who hoped for God's gradual transformation of this age. This pessimism emerged late in Israel, so all the apocalyptic passages are found in the last section of the Hebrew Bible known as "the Writings."

APOCALYPTIC IMAGES IN THE OLD TESTAMENT

EXERCISE 24
Read Daniel 7; 12; Zechariah 9; 14; Malachi 3—4; Joel 1—3; and Isaiah 63:1–6. These passages mark the beginning of apocalyptic thinking. Other passages, such as Isaiah 24—27, are sometimes considered to be apocalyptic.

Daniel is the only real apocalyptic book in the Old Testament, and even then Daniel's visions are confined to the last half of the book (chapters 7—12). The fictional setting places Daniel in exile under King Nebuchadnezzar of Bablyon (1:1), his son Belshazzar (5:1), and an unknown ruler, Darius the Mede (5:31; 9:1). As you know, an apocalypse is often attributed to an ancient figure who claims to predict future events, whereas in fact the author is reading his own view of history back into the past. Daniel falls into this category. His animal visions and their interpretations (7:1–8, 15–27; 8:1–14, 18–26), his analysis of military campaigns (11:2–45), and his references to the desolation of the temple (9:17, 26–27; 11:31; 12:11) serve to date these chapters fairly precisely during the Maccabean Revolution, ca. 165–164 B.C.E. Most commentaries explain these issues in greater detail.[1]

Daniel 7 opens with a dream vision of four beasts emerging from the sea, the symbol of chaos. The focus is on the fourth beast and its most recent king, an eleventh horn. From the description here and in Daniel 8—11 this almost certainly refers to Antiochus IV of Syria, known as Epiphanes, whose brutal campaign against Jerusalem is described in the first chapter of the apocryphal book of 1 Maccabees. To see these passages as predicting events at the end of the twentieth century distorts the whole message of the book. The vision continues as Daniel sees God (the "Ancient of Days") seated on a throne, surrounded by the heavenly council (God's "cabinet") and thousands of others. The beast, and presumably the wicked king, are destroyed and burned (7:11), although we are not told how. Then appears "one like a Son of Man" (7:13). The phrase can mean simply "like a person" or "having a human figure." Here, however, it suggests a cosmic figure. It is the source of the later reflection in 1 Enoch, the Synoptic Gospels, and Revelation 1:13. He receives "dominion and glory and kingship" (7:14) just as the Lamb does in Revelation 5. Since these same attributes are given to the holy ones or saints of the Most High in 7:27, many interpreters feel that the "Son of Man" is a corporate representation of the faithful people. On the other hand, it may refer to the heavenly counterpart or protector of the people, since Michael serves that function (10:13, 21; 12:1; cf. the War Scroll).[2] Even though the Son of Man will establish a new kingdom, along with the saints, nothing in Daniel explicitly says that he wins the victory. He is a cosmic winner without having fought the battle.

In these chapters there is mention of the Kittim (= Rome?) in 11:30. There will be a time of great distress, although those whose names are in the book will be delivered (12:1); a beatitude recognizes those who persevere (12:12). There will be a general resurrection and a final judgment (12:2). Daniel is told to seal up the book until the end arrives (12:4, 9). Despite the cosmic imagery, Daniel's main concerns are the destruction of the wicked ruler, the restoration of the city and the temple, and the fate of those who have been killed for their faith.

When we turn to Zechariah and Malachi, we find a similar situation. The material in Zechariah 9—14 is considerably different from the earlier chapters of the book, in both style and content. Moreover, it consists of two "oracles" (chapters 9—11 and 12—14); and Malachi, which follows immediately, is a third oracle. Apparently Malachi was made a separate book so that the number of minor prophetic books would be twelve, just like the tribes of Israel. The material certainly belongs to the period after the Exile, but it is earlier than Daniel. "Malachi" means "my messenger" and may not be a personal name.

Zechariah 9 is the description of a war in which God is the victor. Paul Hanson describes it as a "Divine Warrior Hymn." It combines the idea of a ritual conquest, familiar to the northern tribes in the period before the monarchy, with the image of a royal procession. Hanson identifies the hymn form in a number of Old Testament passages, including some psalms, which we will not examine.[3] Here, God reconquers the territory promised to Israel (9:1–7) and secures the temple (9:8). Then comes a victory procession, in which God appears to the people as their king and establishes peace among the nations (9:9–10). As we know from recent experience, working out peaceful solutions in international conflicts is no easy task. God then releases captives (9:11–13), appears and celebrates with them at a victory banquet (9:14–15), after which the hymn closes with a picture of abundance after the conquest (9:16–17). Although apparently God will use the tribes in battle (9:13), the victory is God's alone. Note the use of "I" in 9:4, 6–8, 13, and similar sentiments in the third person in verses 10, 14–15. The same theme of God fighting with them and for them appears in 10:5–7.

Zechariah 14 contains a number of themes that reappear in different forms in Revelation. It opens by referring to the day of the Lord (14:1), usually taken to be a day of God's judgment. God gathers the nations against Jerusalem but then intervenes in battle (14:3) along with "all the holy ones," a reference to the angelic hosts as God's army (14:5, reflected in the title "the Lord of hosts" in 14:16–17). Nature will be transformed (14:6–8), although there will be plagues on Israel's enemies and they will panic (14:12–15,

17–19). God, and God's name, will finally be acknowledged as the only king over the whole earth (14:9). The nations will demonstrate their loyalty to Israel's God by coming to Jerusalem to celebrate the festival of booths, one of the most important holy days (14:16). Even ordinary objects such as cooking pots will be purified and dedicated to God (14:20–21). In these passages, then, God is the cosmic victor, and the outcome is a cultic celebration.

In Malachi, the issue is what will happen to the priests and the people who have broken their covenant with God (1—2). A messenger will warn them to prepare for the day of God's coming. It is clearly a day of judgment that should cause terror (3:1–6). The basis for judgment includes personal, social, and cultic violations of the covenant (3:5–15). However, God will remember and reward those whose names are in the book (3:16–18). Once again, the day evokes the image of burning what is not worthwhile (4:1), while the righteous will help judge the wicked (4:2–3). There is no battle imagery here. It is God who acts in judgment. In the closing verses, the prophet Elijah is identified as the one who will return and warn the people of God's coming judgment (4:5–6), an image applied in the Gospels to John the Baptist.

The three short chapters of Joel are prompted by a plague of locusts. It is impossible to date the book with any precision, except that it also belongs to the period after the return from exile. Following the lament in 1:1–13, there is a complex call to repentance marked by a series of refrains: sanctify a fast (1:14), blow the trumpet (2:1), blow the trumpet and sanctify a fast (2:15). The occasion is the impending day of the Lord (2:1, 11), marked by darkness (2:2, 10) and fire (2:3, 10) and earthquakes (2:10). The locusts appear like war horses (2:4), but God appears at the head of an army of hosts (2:11). Once again we find the image of God as warrior combined with the theme of an eschatological judgment. The section 2:28–3:21 is also dominated by the image of the "great and terrible day of the Lord" (2:31; 3:14). That day will be marked by all kinds of natural disasters (2:30; 3:15–16, 19). The day of judgment is payback time. The chosen people will be restored to the land (2:1), Mount Zion will be made secure (3:17, 20), and nature will be turned back to a paradise (3:18). However, the other nations will be punished for what they have done to God's people (3:2–8, 19). The harvest images of the sickle and the winepress, which were developed in Revelation 14:17–20, are found here (3:13). Above all, the passage is a call to arms for other nations to gather against Jerusalem, only to discover that God has an army and sits in judgment (3:9–12). Here also the image of God as judge is fused with that of God as the cosmic victor; the legal and military images coalesce.

The final passage, Isaiah 63:1–6, is consistent with themes we have already noted, but they are exaggerated. God's wrath is almost out of control. God's garments are stained red with the blood of enemies from having trodden the winepress so vigorously. This may be justice, but the image is a rather ruthless one. The military image also asserts that God alone has won the victory without anyone else to help.

From this brief survey, we can see that both the Jewish and the early Christian apocalyptic writers were indebted to a variety of images found in the Hebrew Bible. In addition, a number of even older passages contribute to the "apocalyptic imagination." We need to look at just a sample of them.

PROPHETIC IMAGES
IN THE OLD TESTAMENT

EXERCISE 25
Read Amos 5:18–20; Isaiah 13; Zephaniah 1—3; Ezekiel 38—39; and Psalms 68; 98; 110.

The image of a day of the Lord is an old one, and only gradually was it transformed from a historical judgment against Israel and/or its enemies into a cosmic conflict against all that is evil. In the middle of the eighth century B.C.E. the prophet Amos mentions this concept, although he clearly did not invent it. Quite to the contrary, he was trying to correct a popular view that God's appearing would be a day of joy and celebration. Not at all, Amos claimed; it would be a time of judgment not just on the traditional enemies of the chosen people but also on Judah in the south and Israel in the north (see Amos 1—2). It would be a day of darkness rather than light, of rejection rather than rewards (Amos 5:18–24).

Isaiah was a near-contemporary of Amos, but he lived in Jerusalem and was much more sympathetic to the monarchy. The oracle against Babylon in Isaiah 13 is anachronistic, since Babylon did not become a world power until a century or so after Isaiah. Thus it may be one of his own oracles that was adapted to a later situation, or it may have originated with one of his disciples. Like Amos 5, this passage pictures the day of the Lord as one of punishment and destruction (13:6–9), but in this case it is directed against a hated enemy and even against the whole earth (13:5, 9, 11). God is mustering an army (13:2–5), so the image of God as warrior is prominent here. Unfortunately God's wrath seems uncontrollable (13:6–9, 14–20). Along with the human destruction, there will be enormous ecological disasters (13:10, 13, 21–22). Military imagery dominates this passage.

The superscription of Zephaniah locates him at the end of the seventh century B.C.E., during the time of the Deuteronomic reform (which we will examine in the next chapter) and at the time when Babylon was emerging as the major power in the Middle East. As in Amos and Isaiah 13, the day of the Lord is seen as one of disaster for the whole earth (1:14–18). In this case, God's wrath is directed against Judah (chapters 1; 3) as well as against her enemies (chapter 2). The image of God as warrior (2:12; 3:6, 17) stands alongside verses in which God is calling the nations to judgment (3:5, 8). Ultimately God will deliver those who are faithful, so that they may rejoice (3:14–20); and even foreign nations will change their language so that they may worship Israel's God (3:9–10).[4]

So far we have not paid any attention to Ezekiel, even though it may have had more influence on Revelation than any other Old Testament book. Earlier I suggested that you read the first three chapters of Ezekiel and compare them to the throne vision in Revelation 4 and the scroll scene in Revelation 10. If you did not do it then, you might want to do it now. However, we need to keep our focus on the image of the cosmic victor. In the story of Gog and Magog, which occupies most of Ezekiel 38—39, God demonstrates superiority over Israel's enemies through a series of plagues (38:21–23; 39:6) on the day of judgment (39:7–8). In Revelation, most of these chapters are condensed into a single verse (20:8), except for one powerful image. Wild animals are invited to a sacrificial feast on the flesh and blood of those currently in power (39:17–20). Revelation is more democratic; it extends this invitation to feed on "flesh of all, both free and slave, both small and great" (19:18).

Even though the psalms belong to a different literary genre (neither prophetic nor apocalyptic), they contain many of the same themes. For example, in Psalm 68, God appears as a triumphant warrior (68:17–20). This same God controls nature (68:7–10) and will be worshiped by all nations (68:28–31). God is a cosmic figure, a cloud rider (68:4, 33). Psalm 98 is a song to the God who has triumphed over the nations (98:1–3), who deserves praise from all the people and all of nature (98:4–7), and who will appear to act as a righteous judge (98:9). New Testament writers found a favorite text in Psalm 110:1; but the rest of that passage goes on to celebrate God's military victory and righteous judgment (110:5–6). The theme of God's victory over the kings of the nations of the earth appears in a number of other psalms (e.g., 2:1–3, 10–11; 48:4–11).

What conclusions can we draw from this survey? First, many bizarre images found in the apocalyptic literature, including Revelation, have deep roots in the Old Testament. Second, two of the main images are those of God as judge and as warrior. Third, while the later literature points to an agent of God as the one who wins the victory, in the older sources God acts alone. God acts directly and decisively. God alone is victorious.

QUESTIONS FOR DISCUSSION

1. One of the underlying questions is, "Why do God's chosen people suffer?" Some biblical writers suggest, "You were sinful, so you got what you deserved." Others suggest, "You didn't deserve what happened to you, so God will set things right in the long run." Do you find one of these answers more convincing than the other? If so, why?

2. Before you read this chapter, what did you know about the book of Daniel? If it was familiar to you, did you know more about the early stories (e.g., Daniel in the fiery furnace or in the lion's den) than the apocalyptic chapters? Which half of the book do you think is more relevant today?

3. Does the concept of the "day of the Lord" have any meaning today? If so, how would you explain it to a fifth-grade class?

CHAPTER 12

Holy War, Holy Warrior

We still have not located the biblical source of this military symbolism. Behind the apocalyptic and prophetic visions is another set of images. One is a "holy war," or better, a "war of YHWH," since that term appears in the Bible and "holy war" does not.[1] YHWH, of course, is the personal name of Israel's God, revealed in Exodus 3:14. Second is the "ban" (*ḥerem* in Hebrew), referring to things that are devoted to God or set aside for destruction, so that they are not fit for human consumption. Third is the image of God as warrior. In this chapter we will examine each of the three images and then draw some conclusions.

THE WARS OF YHWH

In 1952, the German scholar Gerhard von Rad published a book exploring the theme of the "holy war" in Israel. It crystallized earlier thinking about that issue, and it laid the foundation for an extended debate that has gone on since then.[2] He identified twelve characteristics of a "holy war," admitting that it was a composite picture and that very few battles included all of these features. For example, we may note the following: trumpets used to summon the army; the consecration of combatants to maintain ritual purity; a charismatic leader who proclaims God's victory; God's presence represented by sacred objects or symbols; psychic warfare (noise, surprise) to cause terror among the enemy; the ban = restrictions on the distribution of the spoils. Above all, these are the wars of YHWH; the enemies are YHWH's enemies.[3] Often God intervenes in a way that brings about the victory. Since von Rad's work appeared, a number of studies have shown that a similar view of war existed among other ancient Near Eastern nations, although their battles tended to be cosmic rather than historical ones. Let us take a look for ourselves at some passages where Israel's view of war is present.

EXERCISE 26

The place to begin is the book of Deuteronomy. Read 7:1–26; 20:1–20; and 21:10–14 to see what these passages say about war and conquest.

In Deuteronomy we once again find a literary fiction. The book claims to record the last words of Moses to the Israelites before they cross over into the promised land. In fact, however, the social situation described throughout the book belongs to a later time. Second Kings 22—23 describes the discovery of a book during repairs to the temple in the reign of Josiah, king of Judah, in 621 B.C.E. That book almost certainly consists of the central chapters of Deuteronomy (chapters 5—26 and 28, with an introduction in 4:44–49). It calls Israel to renew the Mosaic covenant (by obeying its laws, statutes, and ordinances) and to purify its religious practices (by getting rid of local sanctuaries and centralizing worship, presumably at the Jerusalem temple). This purification requires the fervor of an army dedicated to the total destruction of the enemy.

Deuteronomy 7, for example, warns against intermarriage with the inhabitants of the land (7:3–4) and tells the Israelites to destroy local, alien places of worship (7:5, 25). The phrases "utterly destroy them" (7:2) and "set apart for destruction" (7:26) refer to the ban. The theological basis for their action is the covenant. God has freely chosen them and delivered them (7:7–9, 17–19); their response is to keep the commandments (7:11–12). God rewards the obedient and "repays in their own person those who reject him" (7:10). In terms of the ideology of war, the main point is that God acts alone to win the victories for them, just as in the deliverance from Egypt "with a mighty hand" (7:8, 19). God "gives them over" (7:2, 23) and "will clear away these nations" (7:22) and "will hand their kings over to you" (7:24). The presence of God causes panic (7:23).

Deuteronomy 20 makes it clear that when they fight, it is a religious war, not merely a secular battle; this is the biblical basis for the later Crusades. First a priest leads a pep rally and gives them

moral encouragement (20:2–4). Then the officials exempt those re-
cruits who might have any personal distractions, including their
own fear (20:5–9; cf. 24:5). The army of God should be composed
of volunteers. Deuteronomy, like many of the prophets, does not
want people to rely on the standing armies that developed during
the monarchy. When the army defeats a distant town, they are to
kill all the males and take everything else as booty (20:10–15). In
the case of neighboring towns, however, they are to destroy everything, thus removing the temptation to assimilate (20:16–18).
Oddly enough, there is an ecological concern to save all food-bear-
ing trees (20:19–20). In 21:10–14 there are instructions for dealing
with women taken as booty, and in 23:9–14 there are instructions
for maintaining purity during the battle, as we saw in the Qumran
War Scroll. Once again, we must note that it is God who fights for
them (20:4), who gives the victory to them (20:13, 16).

During the late-seventh century B.C.E., when Deuteronomy
was discovered, this model of warfare was unrealistic. The author
or authors were using it for rhetorical purposes to motivate social
and religious reforms. Thus the obvious question becomes, Did
they invent this model, or was there ever a period in Israel's past
where this kind of war was actually fought? Scholars are badly divided in answering that question. What makes it difficult is that
the earlier traditions were collected and edited by writers who
share the Deuteronomic point of view. Let us look at some examples, focusing on the issue of the ban.

THE BAN

EXERCISE 27

Read Joshua 6—8; 1 Samuel 15; and 1 Kings 18. Is the ban carried
out in each case? If not, what happens as a result?

The meaning of the Hebrew term *ḥerem* really depends upon
the context. It some cases it implies that the objects, usually the
booty or spoils of war, are to be totally destroyed, as in Joshua
6:17, 21. Applied to male soldiers, this has the tactical advantage
of removing a military threat. Applied to household objects, it re-
moves the temptation to be seduced by foreign religious or cul-

tural practices. In other cases, however, the term implies that certain objects are to be "devoted" to God, that is, to be set aside and used for cultic purposes (7:18–19, 24).

Joshua 6 is one of the most extended descriptions of a "war of YHWH," complete with the repetitive blowing of the trumpets by the priests, the presence of the ark, and the surprise element of the people shouting. God has given them the city (6:16) without a battle actually having been fought. Of course, there is the intriguing subplot of Rahab, who hid Joshua's spies (Joshua 2) and so she and her family are spared by God (6:17, 22–23, 25). Achan, on the other hand, keeps some of the forbidden booty (7:1). As a result, God refuses to protect Israel when they attack the city of Ai (7:10–12). When confronted, Achan readily admits what he did (7:20–22), but that is not enough. He and everything that belongs to him must be purged in order to restore the covenant relationship (7:22–26). Perhaps more clearly than any other passage, this represents the Deuteronomic perspective on the wars of YHWH. As a result, the raid against Ai is successful, using psychological warfare (8:3–23). The city is totally destroyed (7:24–29), although in this case warriors are allowed to keep some of the spoil for themselves (8:2, 27).

According to 1 Samuel 15, God orders the ban ("utterly destroy all that they have," 15:3) against one of Israel's oldest and most persistent enemies. Saul, the first and tragic king over the northern tribes of Israel, spares the life of Agag, the Amalekite king. He does this for what we would consider the best of reasons: a humanitarian concern for a rival king and a desire to save some of the plunder as a sacrifice to God (15:9, 15). However, his prophetic sponsor Samuel accuses Saul of being disobedient to God. Saul readily confesses what he has done (15:20–21, 24–25), but that does not protect him from divine judgment. He will lose his kingship (15:23, 26), and Agag loses his life (15:33). Here again the Deuteronomic perspective colors the events, especially since we have a different version of Saul's failure in 1 Samuel 13, where as king he preempts Samuel's priestly role by offering a sacrifice.

The last example is that of Elijah, the great ninth-century prophet, who is perhaps the epitome of Deuteronomic obedience to the Mosaic covenant. Elijah challenges the prophets of the Canaanite god Baal and goddess Asherah (1 Kings 18:9) to a contest to see whose god has greater control over nature and can break the drought. After a ceremony that includes some sympathetic magic, YHWH is clearly the winner (18:39), and Elijah proceeds to kill all the Canaanite prophets (18:40). From the Deuteronomic perspective, he is a role model for later Israelites.

In her recent book Susan Niditch examines seven models or ideologies of war within the Hebrew Bible. Two of her chapters deal with two different views of the ban. On the one hand, the ban is seen as "God's portion," that is, as a sacrifice, a tragic but often necessary way of trying to appease God or to gain God's support. A good example is the case of Jephthah in Judges 11. He vows that if God will let him defeat the Ammonites, he will sacrifice the first thing he sees when he returns from battle. He wins, and of course the sacrificial victim turns out to be his own daughter. On the other hand, the ban is often viewed as a way of imposing God's justice on others, of acting as God's agents to destroy whatever God seems to oppose. This view tends to dehumanize. In Niditch's own words, "Enemies are totally annihilated because they are sinners, condemned under the rules of God's justice. . . . The Israelites are to be regarded as God's instruments of justice and the enemy is a less-than-human monster who must be eradicated."[4]

Once again, we return to the question of whether this is an accurate description of the way wars were fought in Israel's past or just an idealized picture. Within the book of Deuteronomy itself and within the Deuteronomic history, the function of the ban image is to whip up a religious fervor, a crusading mentality. We see it today in most terrorist groups, or in extreme pro-life and militia groups, who are so convinced of the righteousness of their cause that they are willing to harass, intimidate, and even kill people with whom they disagree. (Ironically, that was the last sentence I wrote before hearing in the news about the assassination of Israeli prime minister Yitzhak Rabin.)

Without having time or space to defend my answer, I would make the following points. First, the Deuteronomic view of the holy war and the ban is an ideal construct. The Deuteronomic writers did not invent the image, but they did try to bring it back to life and make it the norm by which the covenant people should live. By using it as a filter, they have distorted the pictures of Israel's history in the books of Joshua through Kings. Second, battles did occur before and during the period of the settlement. Some may have been "wars of YHWH," but certainly not all of them were. Third, whether or not battles were seen as "holy wars," Israelites consistently attributed their victories to the fact that God was a warrior fighting for them.

YHWH AS A "MAN OF WAR"

That last sentence finally leads us back to the root image in the Bible, that of God as warrior. The question remains: "How old is that image?" In other words, does it belong to the oldest period of Israel's self-awareness as the people of YHWH?

EXERCISE 28

> Read Exodus 15:1–21, the Song of the Sea (15:1–18) and the Song of Miriam (15:21). Now that you have experience in reading this kind of poetry, what clues help you to understand the structure of the poem? Are there clues that might help you to date it?

Immediately, I have to tell you that experts in the field have answered those questions quite differently. You need to go by your hunches, and then keep reading to learn more about the issues.[5] One school of interpretation sees the poem as ancient, probably in the twelfth century B.C.E. not long after the time of the exodus; another sees its present form as reflecting a time long after the Israelites were settled in their homeland and the temple had become the focal point of their religion. One group interprets the poem in terms of ancient cosmological myths about creation as the conquering of the sea; others see it as an expression of Israel's faith that God acted in history to subdue the Egyptians and free the people of Israel. In its present form, the poem speaks about God's victory at the sea in 15:1–12 (especially 15:5, 10, 12) and God's majesty (15:7, 11). Later verses refer to the settlement in the land of Canaan (15:13–16) and ultimately to God's presence in the sanctuary (the temple) on the holy mount (Zion). There are parallel literary forms in other cultures of the period, but the second half of the poem suggests that its present form took shape during the time of the monarchy.

The most important issue is that the poem reflects the historical experience of the Israelites in the deliverance at the sea. Cosmic elements, if they are present at all, are secondary. God does not conquer the sea; rather, God uses the sea to conquer the Egyptians. Even if the present form of the poem is late, it develops the theme of the Song of Miriam in 15:21, which attributes the victory at the sea to YHWH alone. No battle is mentioned between the Israelite army and the Egyptians. God has won the victory by a miracle, by allowing the sea to submerge the Egyptian chariots. Even if the poem is late, its words reflect an ancient sentiment: "YHWH is a warrior; YHWH is his name" (15:3). Literally the phrase is "YHWH is a man of war." That is reinforced in the poem by references to God's right hand (15:6, 12), themes we have seen in other passages. Apparently, then, this is where the image of the cosmic victor originates—with the exodus experience of God as the one who has delivered the people from bondage and who eventually leads them to the land they claim as their own gift from God. A similar motif appears in the Song of Deborah (Judges 5), one of the oldest poems in the Bible, where God wins the victory by causing a flood that bogs down Sisera and his troops, even though Jael offers the finishing touch by driving a tent peg through Sisera's head!

In part 3 we have taken a detour through some ancient material in order to discover the background of the image of the cosmic victor. What have we learned?

First, the image of God as a "man of war" who fights for Israel appears throughout the Old Testament. In addition to the passages we have studied, the same image appears in Joshua 10:14; Numbers 21:14; Isaiah 42:13 and 59:17; Psalm 24:8; and Habakkuk 3:9. God not only acts in history but also controls the cosmos.

Second, in some passages God acts alone, through surprise or magic, to win the battle. In other passages God cooperates with human agents, including the armies of the people of Israel.[6] In the later apocalyptic literature, some passages (such as the Qumran War Scroll) suggest that the people of God may be involved in actual warfare, while others (such as Ephesians) portray a spiritual battle.

Third, we have seen how this tradition of God as warrior developed in a number of directions. One strand emphasizes the "day of the Lord" as a time of judgment, uniting military and judicial images. Another strand, to which we did not pay much attention, emphasizes the divine council, in which God as king presides over a group of advisers (e.g., Isaiah 6:1–13). In some apocalyptic visions God acts alone, but in others God delegates the victory to a Messiah, a Son of Man, or to a Lamb.[7]

Finally, we have to realize that both images of the "holy war" and of God as a warrior are metaphors. Even in Deuteronomy, the images have a rhetorical function and are not meant to be taken literally. These important issues are ones that we will have to discuss in the final chapters of this book.

QUESTIONS FOR DISCUSSION

1. How do you react to the Deuteronomic picture of the ban? Do you think Christians today should try to destroy everything that they believe God hates?

2. Which view do you find more convincing: that God acts unilaterally in human affairs, or that God cooperates with human beings on their own projects? Why?

3. Based on what you have read so far, do you agree with the message of a bumper sticker that was popular during the Vietnam conflict: "God hates war"? Why or why not?

PART FOUR

Clues for Interpreting Revelation

CHAPTER 13

Misinterpreting Revelation

In this chapter we begin to make a transition. We will deal less directly with biblical and related texts. Rather, we will ask about appropriate ways to interpret those texts. Our focus will still be on the book of Revelation, but in the light of some larger issues. We will look at three misinterpretations of John's imagery: dispensationalism, Christian Reconstructionism, and David Koresh. There are no exercises; instead, there are more notes than for some of the other chapters.

DISPENSATIONALISM

The view that world history can be divided into a series of periods or dispensations is not new, and neither is it unique to the Bible. Today the term "dispensationalism" usually refers to a movement that emerged in the last half of the nineteenth century. It is associated with the work of John Nelson Darby and later Cyrus Scofield, who popularized this point of view through his notes in the Scofield Reference Bible.[1] Dispensationalism is one example of Bible prophecy, the view that every prediction in the Bible must find its fulfillment at some point in human history.[2] It is also one type of premillennialism, the view that Christ's second coming and thousand-year rule (the millennial kingdom) are still in the future.

Dispensationalism has been popularized by Hal Lindsey, whose books have sold millions of copies and have been analyzed in several recent studies.[3] We will focus instead on the writings of John F. Walvoord. His work at the Dallas Theological Seminary covered a period of more than fifty years, including his presidency from 1952 to 1986. During those same years he was editor of their scholarly journal *Bibliotheca Sacra* and published at least fifteen books, many of them appearing in several editions.[4] In other words, as a serious student of scripture he was in a position to influence several generations of church leaders.

Like other dispensationalists, Walvoord's work depends on several basic presuppositions. First, the Bible is inerrant; it contains no historical or factual errors. Second, every biblical prophecy points to God's plan for the future, so it must eventually be fulfilled in a literal way. Third, since all passages of scripture are equally inspired, they can be taken from their original contexts and rearranged to provide a timetable of future events. Fourth, history can be divided into distinct periods or dispensations; the current one is the age of the church. Fifth, all signs point to the fact that we are living in the last period of human history, just before a seven-year period of plagues and wars described in Revelation 6—19 and other apocalyptic passages, known as the great tribulation. Finally, Christians do not need to fear those disasters. Christ will appear secretly and "rapture" genuine Christians from the earth so that they will not have to suffer. That explains bumper stickers such as "In case of the Rapture, this car will be driverless," or watches with the slogan "One Hour Nearer to the Lord's Return." Those who are raptured will live with Christ in heaven until the end of the seven-year period. Then they will return with him and rule with him during the millennium.

In broad outline, dispensationalists argue that predictions in Daniel 7:23–24 and 9:24–27, as well as those in Revelation 6—19, have not yet been fulfilled. They refer to events still in the future. However, the formation of the State of Israel in 1948 and subsequent events have set the whole chain of final events in motion. Signs that Christ is about to return include a thrust toward a "super-church" (the ecumenical movement) and the emergence of a new Roman Empire in the form of a coalition of European nations, based on the need for oil. A new world ruler will emerge in the Middle East and gain control of this coalition. His first act will be to sign a peace treaty with Israel, which will last three and a half years. Then a newly strengthened Russian army will attack Israel, but it will be mysteriously destroyed by divine intervention. The new ruler will demand absolute authority and worship (the Antichrist). For another three and a half years, non-Christians (Israel and Gentiles) will suffer unspeakable horrors, although some Jews will convert to Christianity, as Paul predicted in Romans 11. At the end of that period, there will be another world war, in which two hundred million troops will invade from China, others from Egypt and Africa, and others from Europe. All of them will be totally defeated at the battle of Armageddon, when Christ returns in glory with the saints and establishes his millennial reign. Oddly enough, none of these prophecies apply to the church. This gap is often referred to as "the Great Parenthesis." In other words, biblical prophecies about Israel and the nations apply to world history; prophecies about the church speak only about the marriage to the Lamb in heaven. Dispensationalists have almost nothing to say about the role of the church in America except to wait faithfully for events to be played out in the Middle East.

Let me give just four examples of ways in which Walvoord and others misinterpret scripture, particularly Revelation. First, he insists that John's language must be taken literally whenever possible. However, Revelation—like other apocalyptic books—is full of images and symbols that cannot be taken literally. They cannot be reduced to a single meaning, especially when they are interpreted to refer to particular historical events occurring many centuries in the future.

Second, this same insistence on a literal interpretation is often ignored in dealing with time units. Daniel 9:24–27 speaks of a period of seventy weeks until the fate of Jerusalem has been decided. Although this passage originally referred to the Maccabean revolution, as we have seen, Walvoord and other dispensationalists interpret "weeks" to be "years." The first sixty-nine weeks would lead almost precisely to the death of Christ; but the last "week" of exactly seven years will not begin until the great tribulation, after Christians have been raptured and before Christ's visible return in glory. In the interim, we face a gap of almost two thousand years of church life, about which biblical prophecy has nothing to say. Similarly, Walvoord interprets "five months" in Revelation 9:5 to mean exactly that, whereas "the day of the Lord" refers to an extended time period. He does not think that the phrase "what must take place soon" in Revelation 1:1 refers to the near future; it means simply that when the time comes, events will happen swiftly. So also with the phrase "the time is near" in 1:3. In other words, the literal method is not applied consistently; texts are explained in order to fit the dispensational timetable.

Third, the outline of Revelation is arbitrary, and it distorts the entire message of the book. The key verse is 1:19, in which John is told to write "what you have seen, what is, and what is to take place after this." Walvoord argues that "what you have seen" refers to Revelation 1; "what is" refers to the letters to the seven churches (chapters 2—3); and "what is to take place" applies to the rest of the book. He points out that "church" is not used in chapters 4—18 (in fact, not until 22:16) and that no local congregations are mentioned. On this view, the two witnesses—the woman with her child and the 144,000—do not apply to the church but to Jews who convert during the tribulation period. More important, "The assumption, therefore, that the book of Revelation was understandable in the first generation or that it was intended to be understood by that generation is without real basis."[5] In other words, we understand John better than his original audience did.

Fourth, Walvoord reads into Revelation the concept of the rapture, even though John never mentions it. In 1 Thessalonians 4:17 Paul says that faithful Christians will be "caught up in the clouds" along with the dead in Christ "to meet the Lord in the air"; but Paul refers to the Parousia and the resurrection of believers, not to a secret rapture. Walvoord's view implies a secret coming of Christ to deliver the saints *before* the events described in Revelation 4—19 so that they will not have to suffer during the great tribulation. To support his view, he appeals to the promise to keep the church at Philadelphia from the hour of trial (3:10); but on the basis of the text this promise cannot be extended to all Christians. Also, Walvoord thinks the rapture is prefigured by John's heavenly vision of the 24 elders (4:4) even though it is not explicit in the charge to John to "come up here" (4:1); but that violates Walvoord's own rule to read the text literally. One implication of the dispensational view is that Christians do not need to work for social justice. All they can do is to evangelize so that other people can avoid the coming great tribulation. Keep in mind, however, that there are many other premillennial points of view.

CHRISTIAN RECONSTRUCTIONISM

Christian Reconstructionism, also known as dominion theology, is associated with the work of R. J. Rushdoony, Gary North, Greg Bahnsen, David Chilton, and others. These writers self-consciously, and often vociferously, oppose premillenarianism in general and dispensationalism in particular. In a sense, their debates are intramural, with each side trying to prove the other one wrong.[6] Reconstructionists are postmillennial, saying that Christ's earthly rule began with his death, resurrection, and ascension. In other words, Christ's kingdom coincides with the age of the church. Gradually it will be extended over the whole earth. When that has happened, Christ will return in visible form to exercise his rule. The "millennium" is not meant literally; it simply refers to a long period of time.

The dominion theologians also assume biblical inerrancy, but they are much more open to a symbolic interpretation of some texts, such as the thousand years. However, they insist that biblical passages must be read in their original historical context (often referred to as a "preterist" view). In sharp contrast to dispensationalists, this means that all of John's message was directed to the seven churches; it was not a program for the end of history.

A key to Reconstructionism is the claim that biblical law—the Mosaic law and its interpretation by New Testament writers— should become the law of the land.[7] In other words, it is God's law, not just for Israel, or for the church, which is the new Israel. It reveals God's will for all humanity, for civil society as well as for Christians. The moral decline in our society comes from a failure to keep that law. The goal is to Christianize the world until every state has become a theocracy, based on biblical law. The courts would become religious institutions and would dispense justice based on the moral and case laws of the Mosaic code. This view offers Christians a vigorous, activist role. Basically it says, "Look, you don't need to sit around waiting for the rapture. Here are some things you can do to extend Christ's dominion over the whole earth."

David Chilton has given a Reconstructionist interpretation of Revelation. First, he argues that John's prophecies of coming destruction, like those of Jesus in Matthew 24, were actually fulfilled in the destruction of Jerusalem in 66–70 C.E. Thus he has to argue that the book was written before the fall of the city in order to support his postmillennial position.[8] He is right that John expected disasters to happen in the near future, but that view does not require an early date unless one accepts the book as biblical prophecy. Second, Chilton imposes on Revelation a covenant lawsuit model drawn from the Old Testament. In it, God accuses Israel of having broken the covenant, promises to punish them, and arranges for a successor. According to this model, John identified Babylon as Jerusalem and predicted its fall as Israel's punishment, so that the church would inherit the covenant and the kingdom. Chilton's view supports the negative role that Israel has in dominion theology, but his use of the covenant lawsuit is not convincing. A third misinterpretation is that John expects Christians to rule the world.

> But in principle, and definitively, the Kingdom has arrived. This means that we do not have to wait for some future redemptive or eschatological event before we can effectively take dominion over the earth. The dominion of God's people throughout the world will simply be the result of a progressive outworking of what Christ Himself has already accomplished.[9]

This is a stirring call to involvement in world affairs, but it turns John's view of "persecution ethics" inside out.

DAVID KORESH

The bombing of the Alfred P. Murrah Federal Building in Oklahoma City on April 19, 1995, focused attention once again on the fiery collapse of the Branch Davidian compound in Waco, Texas, exactly three years earlier to the day. The headline of the *Washington Post* on May 28, 1995, was "Waco, the Rise of a Symbol." There is no question that the Branch Davidians, led by David Koresh, had a stockpile of weapons, including illegal ones. There is no question that on February 28, 1993, agents of the Bureau of Alcohol, Tobacco, and Firearms (ATF)—after an investigation of almost ten months—launched an attack on the compound in which four ATF agents and sixteen Branch Davidians died. What was supposed to be a surprise attack turned out to be "Bloody Sunday." This was the beginning of a fifty-one-day siege, the second longest in U.S. law enforcement history. It ended with another attack, in which gas was injected into the compound, which eventually turned the buildings into an inferno. Between 75 and 85 sect members died, including about 25 children. There have been official reports, Congressional hearings, commentaries in the media, and of course books.[10] Our concern here is not to assign blame for the tragic events but to discover how Koresh's thinking was shaped by the Apocalypse.

The movement that led to Koresh (born Vernon Howell in 1959) began with William Miller, who predicted Christ's return in 1843 or 1844. His followers were known as Millerites and eventually became the Seventh Day Adventists. In the 1930s a group in California split and moved to Mt. Carmel, Texas, calling themselves Davidian Seventh Day Adventists. Another split occurred in the mid-1950s, creating the Branch Davidians. After the death of its leader, Howell (who had joined them in 1981) won control of the group. In 1990 he changed his name to David Koresh, reminiscent of the great kings David of Israel and Cyrus of Persia.

At three main points Koresh's interpretation of Revelation was simply wrong. First, he claimed to be the "messenger" of Revelation 10:7, capable of showing how the message on the scroll (Revelation 6—7) applied to him and his followers. Although the Lamb (Christ) had opened the seals, John's prophecies remained unfulfilled until now. Koresh argued that he was a second messiah or messenger from God and the true interpreter of the scriptures. That claim is always a dangerous one, and there is no support for that view in Revelation. Second, Koresh apparently understood the Branch Davidians to be living in the time of the fifth seal in Revelation 6:9–11, awaiting the death of some of their number. James Tabor, one of the few biblical scholars who was able to talk to Koresh, hoped to help him work out a different understanding of the texts. At the time of the final fatal attack, Koresh was working on a manuscript that would explain his understanding of the seven seals and the scroll.[11] Whether he was stalling for time, or whether he would have surrendered when he had finished, remains a contested issue to which we will never know the answer. The third and probably most serious misinterpretation was that Christians were to resist the government by armed force. Koresh originally expected his group to move to Israel and fight in the last great battle. When they came under siege at Mt. Carmel, there is little evidence that they provoked an armed attack so that they could die as martyrs; but they were prepared to defend themselves with weapons, a view that cannot be supported from Revelation.

Each of the three positions we have outlined here deals with many of the same texts, yet they draw strikingly different conclusions. The message of the dispensationalists is, "We're going to miss you." The Reconstructionist's is, "We're going to conquer you," and the Branch Davidian's is, "We're going to fight back." I have tried to suggest, briefly, that our way of reading is largely determined by the assumptions we make and the methods we use. In the remaining chapters we will continue to look at those issues.

QUESTIONS FOR DISCUSSION

1. Your church school superintendent has asked you to take part in a debate on the topic "Resolved: The world is in its last stages of rebellion against God." Would you agree to take part? If so, which side would you represent and what evidence would you present? Find someone to take the other side and see whether you can have a discussion that is both civil and Christian.

2. A large number of Christians view the Bible as a collection of prophecies that must be fulfilled in a literal way. How would you defend that view? How would you criticize it?

3. Dispensationalists suggest that all we can do as Christians is to evangelize, that is, to convert people so that they can escape the great tribulation. Reconstructionists give us a positive program to bring society under the rule of biblical law. Branch Davidians were prepared to use armed resistance against the federal government. Do you find any of these alternatives attractive? Why? If not, what else would you propose?

CHAPTER 14

John's
Historical Context

In chapter 13 we saw how every reading of a text is shaped, at least in part, by the assumptions we make. This book is no exception. In parts 1 and 2, we assumed that we can read Revelation as a literary work of art on its own terms. We can ask questions that we would raise about other literature: style, plot, characters, places, imagery, and so on. Doing so respects John's integrity as an author, by not reading into his book ideas that are not there. It also helps us to understand the world from his perspective. In part 3, on the other hand, we assumed that we should look at other texts with similar ideas. In the New Testament and Jewish apocalyptic passages, we found some of those ideas developed differently. We discovered that John absorbed a lot of Old Testament imagery, even though he almost never footnotes it. When he uses those images, it is fascinating to see how he transforms them. In the rest of part 4, we will assume that Revelation can best be understood in its original historical setting. John explicitly tells us (1:3, 4) that his entire book, not just chapters 2 and 3, applies to the churches in Asia Minor. To understand the context, we want to know who wrote the book and where and when; but we also need to look at the religious/political/social situation the churches faced.

CLUES THAT JOHN GIVES US

Let us review what we learned in our earlier reading of John's book. About himself, he tells us simply that he is a servant of Jesus Christ, a brother to his audience, and that he plays the role of a charismatic Christian prophet. He says that he was on Patmos without really explaining why he was there. None of this helps us to know who John was or when he wrote.

Some commentators have focused on the seven cities. By using historical documents and archaeological evidence, they have given us a much better picture of what it must have been like to live in one of them.[1] Details in the description of Babylon in Revelation 18, particularly its function as an international trade center, obviously refer to Rome, not to Jerusalem.[2] Keep in mind, though, that both cities are highly symbolic for John; we do not exhaust their meaning when we locate them in one particular time and place. Babylon's destruction did come, although not quite in the way John imagined.

We learned about the religious situation of the churches. They faced internal conflicts, tension with the synagogues, and the temptation to worship the emperor. All this could have occurred at any time during the last half of the first century, but two factors point toward the end of that period. Sometime after the fall of Jerusalem, Christianity began to be viewed as a new religion, and Christians were gradually expelled from the synagogues if they had not already left voluntarily. That seems to be the situation here. Also, verses such as Revelation 5:9 and 7:9 imply that Christianity has become global; the Gentile mission is well established.

The political situation cannot really be separated from the emperor cult, as Revelation 13 and 17 demonstrate. The demand for loyalty to the empire and to the emperor was absolute. For John, that demand left Christians no room for compromise. Does he give us any clue to the identity of the emperor at the time he was writing? Yes, he does. John says that the second beast, or more likely the two beasts viewed as one, is a person, the letters of whose name have a numerical value of 666 (13:18). His audience would have had no trouble understanding whom he meant. Unfortunately the original meaning was lost, giving rise to centuries of speculation. In a cartoon strip, Charlie Brown says that Snoopy, his golf partner, got a "6" on the previous hole. "I've got more sixes than the 'Book of Revelation,'" Snoopy replies. Eugene Boring complains about this text's "misuse by calendarizers and religious hobbyists who regard the number 666 as something of a religious crossword puzzle," and rightly argues that the puzzle "challenges the modern interpreter not to historical decoding but to discerning where in our own time propaganda is used to idolize political power."[3] The best solution is that it refers to Nero, who persecuted Christians in Rome and eventually committed suicide. However, many people believed that, like Elvis, he had never really died, or that he would return to life. Then he would head up an army of Rome's traditional enemies to come and destroy the city and the empire. John uses that theory when he tries to explain the puzzle in 17:9–11. Nero is apparently the beast who "was and is not," an obvious parody of God. Nero had died when John wrote, but he would appear again as the eighth ruler (17:11).[4] Even if we cannot identify the precise sequence of events, John expected Nero's reappearance in the near future. What can we conclude from this brief look at the texts? First, they do suggest that John was writing well after 70 C.E. Second, trying to "decode" John's images as though they had only one reference is a waste of time. They have multiple layers of meaning, so they are relevant to us even though John did not have us in mind. For example, Allan Boesak gives a powerful reading of the Apocalypse in the context of the struggle of native Africans for freedom and equality in South Africa.[5]

Another controversial passage deals with the economic aspect of Roman domination. It occurs immediately before the number of the beast is mentioned (13:16–17), and it claims that everyone must have the mark of the beast on the right hand or forehead, otherwise they will not be able to buy or sell. John contrasts these people to the ones who have God's seal on their foreheads (7:3; 14:1). This passage has provided another happy hunting ground for conspiracy theorists. Some see it as a biblical prophecy of a worldwide electronic network through which the Antichrist can control our credit cards, social security numbers, and every other aspect of the economy.[6] There is no way to know precisely what John meant in these verses, but they certainly had to do with the fact that Roman coins carried a picture of the reigning emperor and some kind of inscription about him. Nero's coins, for example, referred to him as "savior of the world." Thus the very currency symbolized the religious and political system that John found oppressive. The clue does not help us at all to date the book.

Finally, John includes a number of references to martyrdom. Remember that the term means "giving witness," but that witness may include giving one's life as well. When John wrote, some Christians had already done so. Nero's brutal persecution of Christians was public knowledge. However, nothing in Revelation suggests that Christians in Asia Minor were being put to death as a matter of state policy. That did happen in the early part of the next century, but Revelation does not fit that setting.

From what we have seen so far, then, John gives us little information to help us pinpoint his historical context. We must look elsewhere.

CLUES THAT OTHERS GIVE US

We cannot review all the evidence, found in most commentaries, from early Christian writers.[7] Most of them believed that the apostle John was the author of Revelation, the Gospel, and the three letters that bear his name. However, the titles of those books came from later tradition, not from the books themselves. In the Fourth Gospel itself the apostle John is never named; the unnamed "Beloved Disciple" is said to have written it (John 21:24). The three letters are similar in style and content to the Gospel, but 2 and 3 John were written by an anonymous "elder" or "presbyter," a title not used by the author of the Apocalypse. Revelation is so different from the other books in style and content that it could hardly have been written by the same person; yet similarities, such as the view of Christ as the Lamb, suggest a common tradition. Even if it could be proven beyond the shadow of a doubt that John knew Jesus personally, that would not enhance the authority with which he speaks, since he claims to have received his message from the risen Christ. We must be content, then, with what John tells us about himself.

The Roman author Pliny says the island of Patmos was used as a penal colony. John's reason for being there, "because of the word of God and the testimony of Jesus" (1:9), has usually been interpreted to mean that he was a prisoner for his religious convictions. Another view is that he was there on a kind of retreat. While meditating, he received the visions recorded in his book. The fact remains that he sent his book in the form of a letter, rather than delivering it in person. This gives some support to the traditional view.

Also, early Christian authors believed that Revelation was written during the reign of the emperor Domitian, thus dating it in the middle 90s of the first Christian century. Nothing in the book itself challenges that date, and much supports it.

To give additional support, many commentators argue that Domitian had an official policy of persecuting Christians in Asia Minor. Twenty years later (ca. 115 C.E.) Pliny, governor of the neighboring province of Bithynia, wrote to the emperor Trajan describing how he dealt with Christians. Those who worshiped the emperor and the images of the gods, and who cursed Christ, were not punished. Those who refused, after a second and third warning, were executed. Until recently, many commentators assumed that Revelation was written in the same kind of setting twenty or so years earlier. However, there is no evidence of an official policy of persecuting Christians at that time, especially in the province of Asia.[8] John's warning about persecution was not a description of the current state of affairs but rather a dramatic warning about what was likely to occur in the immediate future. It was a response to what Adela Yarbro Collins has called a "perceived crisis," and it was intended to reinforce the Christians in their commitment to God and the Lamb.[9]

Christians were very likely harassed and intimidated by neighbors who considered them subversive, but those actions fall far short of a governmental effort to suppress the new religion. If that is so, then the language about persecution and suffering in Revelation does not describe the actual situation of those churches but rather the threat that John believed they would have to face in the near future. He used that threat in order to convince his readers/listeners to be ready to sacrifice their lives for their faith, if that should ever be demanded of them. In other words, Revelation was an apocalyptic tract meant to encourage a group of Christians, alienated from the mainstream of political and ecclesiastical power, to keep their confidence that God would reward their faithful obedience. That was the one thing that gave meaning to their lives.

QUESTIONS FOR DISCUSSION

1. Do you agree with the assumptions stated at the beginning of this chapter? If so, why? If not, how would you change them?

2. How important is it for you to know who John really was? Does it make a difference if he was not actually one of Jesus' twelve disciples?

3. Do you agree with the view that John is describing a "perceived crisis," or do you think that Christians were actually being put to death at the time he wrote? Look for evidence in Revelation to support your position.

CHAPTER 15

Persecution Ethics

How should Christians live? John's answer is only one among the New Testament writers. Rather than appeal to moral principles, he uses military symbols to describe the lifestyle he thinks believers should follow. To understand that lifestyle, then, we need to revisit the images of the holy war (in this chapter) and the holy warrior (in chapter 16).

IMAGES OF VICTORY

EXERCISE 29

By now you probably need an exercise, since you haven't done one for a long time. Review chapters 5—8 in this book, or at least the questions at the end of each chapter. If you are ambitious, reread Revelation 4:1–22:7. What images of conflict and victory do you see that you missed before?

Earlier we traced the image of the holy war back to its roots. Now we need to return to Revelation and see how it is used there. Think of the many symbols drawn from that holy war tradition. Just as the presence of YHWH caused panic among the enemy troops, so the impending presence of God and the Lamb causes panic on the day of their wrath (6:16–17). The trumpets echo the fall of Jericho; remember also their prominent place in the War Scroll. At the blowing of the last trumpet God's ark becomes visible (11:19). The plagues recall God's control over nature in Exodus, particularly at the crossing of the sea. We should not be surprised when the ones who have conquered the beast sing the Song of Moses (a reminder of Exodus 15 and also of Deuteronomy 32, which we did not look at). Other victory celebrations occur after the blowing of the seventh trumpet (11:15–17), the defeat of the dragon (12:10–12), and the destruction of the city (19:1–5). The holy war imagery can also explain a number of other peculiar features in Revelation.[1]

In chapter 8, we looked at the climactic scene in Revelation 19:11–21. Look at it again now. First John gives us a description of the rider on the white horse, including the fact that he wears a robe dipped in his own blood (19:13). Next we meet his armies. They are wearing pure white linen and, like him, are riding white horses (19:14). Who are these armies? Many commentators take them to be angels, the heavenly host of the Old Testament. John, however, has transformed this vision of the army and has given us a number of clues to identify the troops. In 6:9–11, the souls of the martyrs—quite likely Christians whom Nero had put to death—are given white robes until their number is complete. In 7:1–8 we learn that the number of those to be sealed is 144,000. This is not a fixed number but a symbol of completeness ($12 \times 12 \times 1,000$) for the church as the new Israel. Then we meet a great multitude from every geographic and ethnic group who have washed their robes in the blood of the Lamb to make them white (7:14). The blood and the white robes clearly link this group to Christ and his army in 19:13–14. In 17:14, a verse that prepares us for the final battle, we are explicitly told that those with the Lamb are "called and chosen and faithful." Christ's "armies" in 19:14, then, are Christians who have given their lives for his sake. They will be the real winners in the cosmic battle against the forces of evil. On the other hand, when we meet the 144,000 again in 14:1–5, they are standing with the Lamb on Mount Zion, that is, on earth. Apparently their number is now complete. The fact that "they have not defiled themselves with women" (14:4) is not a demand for permanent celibacy. As we saw in the Old Testament and in the War Scroll, soldiers must resist idolatry and remain pure while the holy war is fought. They represent the church, those Christians who are called to do battle with the beast. They serve as the earthly counterpart of the heavenly army. Apparently they share in the first resurrection (20:4–6).

HOW SHOULD CHRISTIANS FIGHT?

According to John, how should Christians live? A complete answer to that question would require another book, so we will focus on his view of the Christian life as warfare, a life-and-death conflict with the forces of evil in our world. Because this metaphor is so easily misinterpreted, we must look carefully at how John thinks Christians should fight.

1. Christians are called "to conquer." As we have already seen, in each of the letters to the seven churches the risen Christ makes a different promise. In every case, however, the promise is made "to everyone who conquers." Near the end of the book, after John has seen the new heaven and the new earth, the figure on the throne promises an inheritance to "those who conquer," including the promise to be their God (21:7). This is one of the few passages in which God is quoted directly. But what does it mean to conquer?

Christ provides the model for Christian living. As the "Lion of the tribe of Judah, the Root of David" he has conquered so that he is able to open the scrolls (5:5). That is messianic language, normally used in Jewish literature for an earthly king who would triumph over Israel's enemies and establish God's rule on earth. John transforms this messianic image. For one thing, Christ's victory is not over the Romans but over the cosmic forces of evil. It is not until the final battle that the reign of Christ and God will be established on earth (17:14; 19:11–20:10). For another thing, Christ's victory is won not on the battlefield but on the cross. He was dead but now is alive forever (1:18). He was the Lamb who was slaughtered (5:6). If Christians expect to conquer, they must follow his example and be willing to die. There is no dominion theology in Revelation.

In fact, John reports that some Christians have conquered Satan "by the blood of the Lamb and by the word of their testimony, for they did not cling to life even in the face of death" (12:11). Those who sing the Song of Moses have "conquered the beast and its image and the number of its name." As a result, John sees them standing in heaven beside the sea of glass (15:2), meaning that they conquered by losing their lives.

At the same time, John realizes that a demonic use of power may involve great human suffering, as in the case of the first rider who comes to conquer (6:2). The beast from the pit "will make war on them [the two witnesses] and conquer them and kill them" (11:7), while the beast from the sea "was allowed to make war on the saints and to conquer them" (13:7). In both of these cases Christians are victims. They may suffer violence, but they are not to use it.

By "conquering," then, John did not mean the use of weapons or even of political power.² For him, the beasts symbolize the tendency of human institutions to become corrupt and unjust. His greatest fear was that Christians would cooperate with them, even though his churches were relatively powerless. He did not anticipate a time when Christians would exercise imperial power or become a majority in a nation; but he would not be surprised that Christians might also use power ruthlessly and demonically. We might think of the Spanish conquest of Latin America or of the Holocaust in Germany or of the treatment of slaves and Native Americans in this country or of massive industrial pollution.

2. Another mark of a Christian's lifestyle is to bear witness. The Greek stem *martur-* in its various forms occurs nineteen times in Revelation. It gives us our word "martyr," although the basic meaning is to testify or give witness. In the NRSV the noun form is usually translated "testimony."

In some passages, particularly in the opening and closing sections of the book, it is not clear whether it refers to testimony from Jesus or about Jesus (e.g., 1:2, 9; 22:16, 18 [translated "warn"], 20; also twice in 19:10). Probably John had both senses of the phrase in mind, since what the Christians had to say about Christ was what they had heard from him.

Once again Jesus provides the model for Christian behavior. He is the "faithful witness" (1:5), the "faithful and true witness" (3:14). He also testifies to the things written in John's book, in effect vouching for their accuracy (22:20). His witness includes his words, the message delivered to Christian prophets. It also includes his work, that is, his death. His willingness to die for the word of God establishes the pattern that Christians are to follow.

John also characterizes himself as one who has testified (1:2, 9), so that he too becomes a role model. In 19:10, where the testimony of Jesus is identified with the spirit of prophecy, an angel rejects John's worship on the ground that he simply holds the testimony of Jesus, like the other Christian prophets. In 19:9–10, John may be warning the churches against the worship of angels, which was a temptation for Christians in Asia Minor.

Revelation has a long list of faithful witnesses; they provide additional examples for the churches to follow. Antipas is one of them (2:13). The fact that he gave his life is not important for its own sake. What really matters is the reason for his death, the fact that he remained a faithful witness to Jesus' own death and subsequent triumph. Most of the other examples are also people who were willing to accept death as a result of their testimony: the souls of those who had been slain (6:9); the two witnesses (11:7); those who "loved not their lives even unto death" (12:11, RSV); those whose blood made Babylon drunk (17:6); "the souls of those who had been beheaded for their testimony to Jesus and for the word of God" (20:4). The woman's children are being pursued by the dragon, but they "keep the commandments of God and hold the testimony to Jesus" (12:17). For John, that is a condensed summary of the Christian lifestyle. It is a kind of "grace under pressure," an unwillingness to conform to the surrounding culture. That, in turn, involves a conflict of religious and political loyalties.

3. In the face of those conflicts, Christians must resist. One term that John uses to convey this idea is *thlipsis*. Older translations used the English word "tribulation." More recent translations prefer "affliction," but the term has a range of meanings. In the letters to the seven churches it appears three times (2:9, 10, 22). It is also used in 1:9, where John claims to be a partner in their suffering or distress. Since there is no evidence of persecution by Roman officials, John was trying to prepare his audience for the worst that might happen to them. In the body of Revelation, the term is used only in 7:14, referring to those who have "come out of the great ordeal."

Another of John's favorite terms is *hypomene*, usually translated as "patience" or "endurance" or "patient endurance." It is used in letters to the churches at Ephesus (2:2,3), Thyatira (2:19), and Philadelphia (3:10), where they are praised for their perseverance. Elsewhere the term appears in a crucial passage. John has just introduced the first beast, with its claim to world power and its demand for universal worship. After warning his audience against using the sword, John tells them, "Here is a call for the endurance and faith of the saints" (13:10). The other passage in Revelation comes between the vision of the 144,000, the three angels who warn against idolatry, and the last judgment scene. In that context, John says again, "Here is a call for the endurance of the saints, those who keep the commandments of God and hold fast to the faith of Jesus" (14:12). They must refuse to worship the emperor or to receive the mark of the beast.

The mark of the beast had to do with buying and selling, not just with worship (13:16–18). Since that mark appeared on Roman coins, one plausible explanation is that John was telling Christians to resist using those coins. That would certainly put them at a disadvantage in the marketplace. It would be consistent with John's other warnings against the seductiveness of wealth.[3]

Revelation, then, is a subversive book. John is a prophetic voice calling Christians to nonviolent resistance. They are not to use weapons or fight back. Yet they must refuse to cooperate with corrupt institutions in society. They must give witness to their faith at the risk of their own lives. John's message was largely for people whom we would consider marginalized, without power or influence. Today, when Christians control so much power and wealth, John would warn us not to be corrupted by idolatry. He would be less concerned with reshaping the world than with shaping Christian behavior. On controversial issues such as abortion and public prayers and violence in the media he would be less interested in public policy than in the way Christians deal with those issues within the life of the church. He would certainly challenge Christians for whom gun ownership defines personal freedom and personal identity. Ironically, the holy war imagery turns out to be a protest against violence in any form.

QUESTIONS FOR DISCUSSION

1. Is the appeal of Revelation only to people who are oppressed or "marginalized," or does it have something to say to people in power? Give some examples to support your view.

2. Do you agree with John's view that Christians should suffer violence but not inflict it on others? Explain why you agree or disagree.

3. Could John have made a more convincing argument if he had not used the imagery of the holy war?

CHAPTER 16

John's
Theological Vision

In teaching college undergraduates and adult Bible classes, I learned that many Christians today have never read the passages about God as a warrior and the wars of YHWH, and the first response of most Christians is to find the images offensive. Isn't God pictured as a jealous, vindictive Middle Eastern potentate? Is this image of God, and John's image of Christ as the cosmic victor, really consistent with our Christian faith? You may share some of those feelings. Our final task is to look more closely at some objections that have been raised about John's theology and then to see how we might answer them.

SOME CONSCIENTIOUS OBJECTIONS

1. One criticism compares the Old Testament picture of God as warrior with the New Testament picture of a loving God. It argues that Jesus and the early church replaced an inferior militaristic image of God with the image of God as a loving Father. Since John is so dependent on the holy war tradition, his theology is viewed as inferior to that of the rest of the New Testament.

2. A more specific objection appeared during the 1980s, when people faced the prospect of a nuclear war. Read, for example, the words of Carol Christ, a leading feminist theologian and peace activist:

> The God of Exodus and the Prophets is a warrior God. My rejection of this God as a liberating image for feminist theology is based on my understanding of the symbolic function of a warrior God in cultures where warfare is glorified as a symbol of manhood and power.[1]

In addition to reinforcing male aggression and domination, she argues, the symbol of a warrior God also promotes religious intolerance. Similarly, Daphne Hampson rejects the traditional monotheistic concept of a God who is transcendent, all-powerful, and self-sufficient.[2] Many other women share the same view.

3. Tina Pippin presents a different feminist argument, using a complex combination of literary analysis, psychological insights, and an appreciation for fantasy.[3] She argues that Revelation presents women as objects of desire, who must either be destroyed violently (Jezebel, Babylon the whore) or violated (the Bride/city who is entered by the faithful, all of whom are male). This treatment of women is a kind of scapegoating, and it provides a catharsis for those who are politically repressed. Pippin rejects this portrayal of women as unacceptable.

4. Arthur Mendel has attacked apocalyptic imagery because it tends to promote violence in social and political life.[4] His book is basically a survey of apocalyptic movements in Western history, from the Hebrew prophets and Greek thinkers to contemporary fundamentalism. The Crusades, medieval millenarian movements, the French and Russian revolutions, Hitler, and the "flower children" have all sought to transform this world according to some model of apocalyptic bliss. In contrast, Mendel calls us to return to the this-worldly focus of the early biblical writers and the prophets, so that we might recover the values of justice and peace.

5. Finally, there is the opposite charge, that apocalyptic thinking is escapist. It is pie-in-the sky dreaming that leads individuals to focus on their own personal salvation, neglecting their social, political, and cultural environment. This applies to John's persecution ethics only in the sense that Christians do not try to revolt against Roman oppression, but they are certainly not passive in their refusal to conform to Roman religious and political values.

THE RELEVANCE OF JOHN'S THEOLOGY

Central to John's message is his view of God as remote and exalted, yet deeply concerned with the future of the faithful community. His view has been profoundly shaped by the metaphor of God as a warrior and associated images, such as the holy war and the day of YHWH. Yet John's theology is basically a Christology. In other words, everything that the Old Testament says about God is transferred to, or shared with, the Lamb. Recall how both share the throne and the kingdom, the power and the glory. That is especially true of the image of God as warrior and judge. In Revelation, it is the Lamb who carries out the last judgment (14:14–20) and wins the final battle (19:11–21). The Lamb is not simply an agent of God, like the messiah in some apocalyptic literature, but God's alter ego. The image of the warrior God has been transformed into that of the victorious Christ.

John makes an even more profound transformation of the biblical images when he says that Christ's real victory was won on the Cross. That is when the powers of Satan were defeated. All that remains is for his victory to be won "on earth, as it is in heaven." On the Cross, Jesus shows us what it means to conquer and to be a witness: It means to be willing to give your life for the word of God. Our ordinary understanding of violence as the exercise of power is reversed, with the victim becoming the victor. When we reply to criticisms of John's theology, it is from that point of view.

There are several points to make in reply to the first two objections presented above. First, ever since Marcion rejected the Old Testament as inferior in the middle of the second century C.E., the church has refused to accept that view. Such a view leads to a kind of anti-Semitism. Second, the image of a loving and caring God is found in both testaments, just as the images of warfare and judgment and ultimate victory are found in both. Each testament contains a variety of images of God. If we simply discard the ones we don't like, then we distort the biblical witness and shrink our imaginations. Third, if we delete all the passages that refer to God as warrior, as the church has often done, it becomes difficult to talk about God as our creator, as liberator, and as the one who gives us hope.[5] Fourth, it is important to see that John has toned down the violent imagery. God remains the ultimate source of power, but God does not intervene directly in human affairs. Instead, God acts through intermediaries: angels, the Son of man, the Lamb, and so on. As one commentator says about the plagues, "Thus the way John portrays the judgments is as far as possible from the image of a human despot wielding arbitrary power."[6] Despite the vivid images of destruction in other passages, John never describes an actual battle between the Lamb and the kings of the earth.[7] In 17:16, it is actually the patron kings who will turn and destroy Babylon. Violence is ultimately self-destructive.

As for the third criticism, by Tina Pippin and others, it is true that John describes Babylon as a prostitute who seduces Christians into false worship and immoral behavior. That image is regrettable, but it is part of a tradition that goes all the way back to the Hebrew prophets (particularly Hosea in the eighth century B.C.E.). The basic issue of interpretation is whether we can condemn John on the basis of modern feminist theory or whether he was using stock images his readers would have understood. If John had introduced a new set of symbols, would his audience have understood his message?

In response to Mendel's criticism, he is absolutely correct that apocalyptic fervor has often led to violence, whether driven by religious or political motives. That has happened especially when John's images are taken as a literal blueprint for a revolution or a religious reform. Nevertheless, those images make at least two points that are essential to the Christian faith. One is that evil is pervasive. In our personal lives, there are things we cannot always control, such as addiction or anger. In our social life, we confront events, such as poverty and graft and riots, that are beyond the control of a Congress, a dictator, or even a church. There is an unseen power that seems to corrupt even the best people and the best plans. Satan and the beasts symbolize that cosmic dimension of evil. The second affirmation is that God is just and will ultimately win out over the forces that seek to destroy human life. Without that affirmation, life seems to be chaotic and meaningless. We have no way, of course, to prove that God and the Lamb will eventually win. We cannot describe what is beyond human experience. John's visions are important not because they tell us when the Lamb's victory will occur or how it will happen but only that it will happen.

TRANSLATING JOHN'S IMAGERY

We need to tie up some loose ends and bring part 4 to a close. John presents us with a kaleidoscope of images. What is the best way to make sense of them? How should we relate his imagery to our own lives?

First of all, there are some methods to avoid. (1) Avoid *literalism*. Don't assume that each image has to have a single meaning or that every plague and battle has to happen exactly as it is described. On the contrary, every earthquake and every famine is a reminder to repent. Every war and every drive-by shooting is a reminder of the demonic power that drives people to destroy other human

lives. When John describes Babylon, he is not asking you to picture a woman in hot pants standing on a street corner. Rather, he
wants you to realize how seductive wealth and luxury can be.
When he writes about a new Jerusalem coming down from
heaven, he does not mean that somewhere in outer space there is
a city floating around just waiting to come to earth in Israel.
Rather, he asks you to picture what human life would be like without crime and hatred.

(2) Avoid *triumphalism*, the view that God is going to reward us
and destroy everyone who doesn't agree with us. The image of a
last judgment or a final battle symbolizes God's ultimate victory
over human sin in all its forms. It is so easy for us to identify ourselves as those who conquer and to identify the beast as persons or
groups who disagree with us. That is too easy a temptation because we are the ones who are being tested.

(3) Avoid using *violence*. Revelation describes a world in which
there is a great deal of violence. Some of it is a result of natural
disasters. Some of it is caused by human beings who want to dominate and oppress other human beings. Some of it may be directed
against the Christians to whom John was writing, as well as against
all who fear God's name (e.g., 5:9; 11:18). Never once, though,
does Revelation suggest that Christians can use violence against
anyone else, even in retaliation.

Second, there are also some steps to take if you are really going
to understand and appreciate John's message. (1) Above all, *use your
imagination*. When I was growing up, one of my grandmothers used
to express her surprise by saying "Just imagine" or some variation
of that phrase. If she had been alive, for example, when the first as-
tronaut set foot on the moon, her response would have been, "Well,
imagine that!" Marcel Proust once said, "The real voyage of discovery consists not in seeking new lands, but in seeing with new
eyes."[8] John invites us to explore his landscape with ears and eyes
open, to take advantage of the virtual reality that he offers.

(2) Revelation also challenges us to *resist evil*. For John, that
meant refusing to participate in activities, either religious or civic,
that recognized the authority of the emperor. Today, identifying
the sources of evil and knowing how to resist them is much more
complicated. It may involve helping your church establish a shel-
ter for abused women or working to prevent child abuse or serv-
ing in a food kitchen for the homeless. John does not give us a

script but invites us to use our imaginations so that we can discover how best to bear witness and resist evil.[9]

The message of Revelation, in the words of the cab driver, is that "God wins." Christ is victorious.

QUESTIONS FOR DISCUSSION

1. Do you sympathize with some of the objections to John's theology? Are there other objections you would have raised? If so, how would you answer them?

2. What would you add to the brief description of John's views of God and the Lamb?

3. Do you agree with the lists just given of methods to avoid and steps to take when translating John's theology? Are there other points you would add to either list?

NOTES

Chapter 1. Revelation as a Multimedia Event

1. Elisabeth Schüssler Fiorenza, *Revelation: Vision of a Just World*, Proclamation Commentaries (Minneapolis: Fortress Press, 1991), 31.
2. See David Aune, *Prophecy in Early Christianity and the Ancient Mediterranean World* (Grand Rapids: Wm. B. Eerdmans Publishing Co., 1983); also see C. Freeman Sleeper, *The Bible and the Moral Life* (Louisville, Ky.: Westminster/John Knox Press, 1992), 55–65.
3. Following earlier studies by Frederic Palmer and John Wick Bowman, James L. Blevins, *Revelation as Drama* (Nashville: Broadman Press, 1984), developed an elaborate scheme for a public performance. More convincing is an article by David Barr, "The Apocalypse of John as Oral Enactment," *Interpretation* 40 (1986): 243–56.
4. Many of John's visions occur when he is "in the spirit": 1:10; 4:2; 17:1; 21:9. In 14:13, a voice from heaven commands him to write, followed by the voice of the Spirit in the next verse. The Spirit and the bride (Christ) are mentioned together in 22:17.

Chapter 3. The People

1. This point has been developed by Tina Pippin in *Death and Desire: The Rhetoric of Gender in the Apocalypse of John* (Louisville, Ky.: Westminster/John Knox Press, 1992), esp. chap. 5, "Fantasy and the Female: The Ideology of Desire," 69–86.
2. In 1 Corinthians 16:22, the prayer "Our Lord, come!" is *Marana tha*, a transliteration from the Aramaic. This indicates that the

prayer belonged to the earliest years of the church, before Greek became the predominant language.

Chapter 4. The Places

1. This has been vividly demonstrated by Adela Yarbro Collins in her doctoral dissertation, published as *The Combat Myth in the Book of Revelation* (Missoula, Mont.: Scholars Press, 1976).

2. Sir William Ramsey explored the daily life of these cities in *The Letters to the Seven Churches of Asia* (London: Hodder & Stoughton and Armstrong, 1904). More recently, Colin J. Hemer, *The Letters to the Seven Churches of Asia in the Local Setting*, JSNT Supplement Series 11 (Sheffield: JSOT Press, 1986), has tried to relate every detail in Revelation 2—3 to the sociopolitical situation of Asia Minor.

Chapter 5. The Dimensions of Conflict

1. Revelation 18:20 links the fall of Babylon to God's vindication of "saints and apostles and prophets," while 21:14 suggests that the names of the twelve apostles are written on the foundations of the new Jerusalem.

2. Some Corinthian Christians apparently had a similar attitude. They justified eating food from the local market with the slogan "All things are lawful" (1 Corinthians 10:23–30). The same slogan appears in 1 Corinthians 6:12, followed by a discussion of food and fornication—the same two issues mentioned in Revelation!

3. For a condensed discussion of these issues, see Leonard Thompson, *The Book of Revelation: Apocalypse and Empire* (New York: Oxford University Press, 1990), 158–67. Most commentaries also include a discussion of the topic.

4. By contrast, Marla J. Selvidge's article "Powerful and Powerless Women in the Apocalypse," in *Neotestamentica* 26 (1992): 157–67, seems to assume that John deliberately used this imagery in order to put down women who were independent and had power of their own.

Chapter 6. Images of Natural Catastrophes

1. J. Massyngberde Ford, *Revelation*, Anchor Bible 38 (Garden City, N.Y.: Doubleday & Co., 1975), 112.

2. See, e.g., John M. Court, *Myth and History in the Book of Revelation* (Atlanta: John Knox Press, 1979), esp. 48–51.

3. The Greek word translated "tribulation" in older versions appears in Revelation, but in the NRSV it is translated as "persecu-

tion" in 1:9, as "affliction" in 2:9–10, as "distress" in 2:22, and as "ordeal" in 7:14.

4. Richard Bauckham has done an illuminating study of "The Eschatological Earthquake" in an article now incorporated in *The Climax of Prophecy* (Edinburgh: T. & T. Clark, 1993), 199–209.

5. Paul S. Minear, *I Saw a New Earth* (Washington, D.C.: Corpus Books, 1968), argues provocatively that the real purpose of the plagues is to test Christians, not outsiders. Are they able to remain faithful in the face of both internal and external threats?

Chapter 7. Images of Military Conflict

1. Isbon T. Beckwith, *The Apocalypse of John* (Grand Rapids: Baker Book House, reprinted 1967; original copyright Macmillan Co., 1919), 638.

Chapter 8. The Cosmic Victor

1. The only other place where Christ is described as "the Word" is in the Prologue to John's Gospel (1:1–18). Even if both books are not by the same author, the identification of Christ as the Word and as the Lamb is found in the New Testament only in these books.

2. Curiously, John speaks of a "first resurrection" and a "second death," but he does not use the term "second resurrection" even though he describes one.

Chapter 9. The New Testament Context

1. For a technical but readable discussion, see Ralph Martin, *Colossians and Ephesians*, New Century Bible (Greenwood, S.C.: Attic Press, 1974), 8–19, esp. 10–14.

2. On the language of power, see C. Freeman Sleeper, *Black Power and Christian Responsibility* (Nashville: Abingdon Press, 1969), 118–46; Clinton E. Arnold, *Ephesians: Power and Magic* (Grand Rapids: Baker Book House, 1992); and Walter Wink, *Unmasking the Powers* (Philadelphia: Fortress Press, 1986), esp. 128–52 on "the elements." This was the first in a trilogy by Wink on the powers and their implications for today.

Chapter 10. The Jewish Apocalyptic Context

1. A good place to begin is Menahem Mansoor, *The Dead Sea Scrolls*, 2d ed. (Grand Rapids: Baker Book House, 1983), or Geza Vermes, *The Dead Sea Scrolls in English*, 4th ed. (New York: Penguin U.S.A., 1995). Early works are Millar Burrows, *The Dead Sea Scrolls* (New

York: Viking Press, 1955), and Geza Vermes, *Discovery in the Judean Desert* (New York: Desclée Co., 1956).

2. Excellent summaries of the content are found in Mansoor, *The Dead Sea Scrolls*, 57–68, and in Yigael Yadin, *The Message of the Scrolls* (London: Weidenfeld & Nicolson, 1957), 128–43. The definitive study is also by Yadin, *The Scroll of the War of the Sons of Light* (London: Oxford University Press, 1962). As both a teacher of archaeology at the Hebrew University in Jerusalem and a general in Israel's 1948 war for independence, Yadin was uniquely prepared to interpret this scroll.

3. Richard Bauckham explores this analogy in an article reprinted as "The Apocalypse as a Christian War Scroll," in *The Climax of Prophecy* (Edinburgh: T. & T. Clark, 1993), 210–37.

4. Yadin, *The Message of the Scrolls*, 130.

5. John J. Collins, *The Apocalyptic Imagination* (New York: Crossroad, 1987), 133.

6. See, e.g., Collins, *The Apocalyptic Imagination*, 1–32. The rest of the book is a good discussion of relevant texts.

7. A convenient collection of readings, along with explanatory comments, is Mitchell G. Reddish, *Apocalyptic Literature: A Reader* (Nashville: Abingdon Press, 1990). Charles H. Talbert, *The Apocalypse* (Louisville, Ky.: Westminster John Knox Press, 1994), urges that one read these texts before looking at Revelation. I have reversed that approach.

Chapter 11. The Old Testament Context

1. See, e.g., W. Sibley Towner, *Daniel*, Interpretation 23 (Atlanta: John Knox Press, 1984).

2. For a brief survey of different opinions, see Towner, *Daniel* 104–6, and John J. Collins, *The Apocalyptic Imagination* (New York: Crossroad, 1987), 78–85.

3. Paul D. Hanson, *The Dawn of Apocalyptic*, rev. ed. (Philadelphia: Fortress Press, 1979), 292–401, esp. 292–324.

4. Elizabeth Achtemeier, *Nahum-Malachi*, Interpretation 24 (Atlanta: John Knox Press, 1986), 66–67, gives a convenient summary of the way this concept is used in the Old Testament. A review of the scholarly literature is found in Michael S. Moore, "Yahweh's Day," *Restoration Quarterly* 29 (1987): 193–208.

Chapter 12. Holy War, Holy Warrior

1. In 1 Samuel 18:17 and 25:28 the NRSV translates the phrase as "the battles of the LORD." Numbers 21:14 actually quotes from "the Book of the Wars of the LORD."

2. Gerhard von Rad, *Holy War in Ancient Israel*, trans. Marva J. Dawn (Grand Rapids: Wm. B. Eerdmans Publishing Co., 1991). This edition contains a thirty-page summary by Ben C. Ollenburger of the recent debate and a twenty-seven-page annotated bibliography by Judith E. Sanderson.

3. *Ibid.*, 41–51.

4. Susan Niditch, *War in the Hebrew Bible* (New York: Oxford University Press, 1993), 152.

5. For a balanced survey of the issues, see James Watts, *Psalm and Story*, JSOT Supplement Series 139 (Sheffield: JSOT Press, 1992).

6. Millard C. Lind, *Yahweh Is a Warrior* (Scottdale, Pa.: Herald Press, 1980), emphasizes God's solo performances, thus playing down the role of military exploits. Patrick D. Miller, in a number of articles and especially in *The Divine Warrior in Early Israel* (Cambridge, Mass.: Harvard University Press, 1973), stresses the "synergism" between God and Israel.

7. A recent book by Tremper Longman III and Daniel Reid, *God Is a Warrior* (Grand Rapids: Zondervan Publishing House, 1995), traces the image of God as warrior through the Bible in five stages, roughly corresponding to what we have just done in a reverse sequence.

Chapter 13. Misinterpreting Revelation

1. For a survey of the broader issues, see Timothy P. Weber, *Living in the Age of the Second Coming*, enl. ed., Academie Books (Grand Rapids: Zondervan Publishing House, 1983); Paul Boyer, *When Time Shall Be No More* (Cambridge, Mass.: Harvard University Press, Belknap Press, 1992), esp. 80–112; and George M. Marsden, *Understanding Fundamentalism and Evangelicalism* (Grand Rapids: Wm. B. Eerdmans Publishing Co., 1991).

2. J. Barton Payne, *Encyclopedia of Biblical Prophecy* (New York: Harper & Row, 1973), is a comprehensive survey of passages that point to some future event.

3. Lindsey's best-sellers are *The Late Great Planet Earth* (New York: Bantam Books, 1973), and *The 1980's: Countdown to Armageddon* (New York: Bantam Books, 1981). For an analysis of his arguments, see Stephen D. O'Leary, *Arguing the Apocalypse: A Theory of Millennial Rhetoric* (New York: Oxford University Press, 1994), esp. 134–71.

4. Among Walvoord's major works, see *The Millennial Kingdom*, Academie Books (Grand Rapids: Zondervan Publishing House, 1959); *The Rapture Question*, rev. and enl. ed. (Grand Rapids:

Zondervan Publishing House, 1979); his scholarly study *The Revelation of Jesus Christ* (Chicago: Moody Press, 1969; paperback ed. 1989); and his popular *Armageddon: Oil and the Middle East Crisis*, rev. ed. (Grand Rapids: Zondervan Publishing House, 1990; orig. ed. 1974).

5. Walvoord, *The Revelation of Jesus Christ*, 23.
6. A thoughtful analysis and critique from a dispensational viewpoint is H. Wayne House and Thomas Ice, *Dominion Theology: Blessing or Curse?* (Portland, Oreg.: Multnomah, 1988).
7. The most extensive treatment is R. J. Rushdoony, *The Institutes of Biblical Law* (Phillipsburg, N.J.: Presbyterian and Reformed Publishing Co., 1973); see also Greg Bahnsen, *Theonomy in Christian Ethics* (Phillipsburg, N.J.: Presbyterian and Reformed Publishing Co., 1977).
8. David Chilton, *The Days of Vengeance* (Fort Worth, Tex.: Dominion Press, 1987). A stronger defense of the early date is Kenneth L. Gentry, Jr., *Before Jerusalem Fell* (Tyler, Tex.: Institute for Christian Economics, 1989).
9. Chilton, *Days of Vengeance*, 69.
10. See esp. James R. Lewis, ed., *Making Sense of Waco* (Lanham, Md.: Rowman & Littlefield Publishers, 1994).
11. A copy of Koresh's interpretation of the first seal is included in James D. Tabor and Eugene V. Gallagher, *Why Waco?* (Berkeley: University of California Press, 1995), 191–203.

Chapter 14. John's Historical Context

1. Sir William Ramsey reported on the daily life of these cities in *The Letters to the Seven Churches of Asia* (London: Hodder & Stoughton and Armstrong, 1904). Colin J. Hemer uses more recent discoveries in *The Letters to the Seven Churches of Asia in the Local Setting*, JSNT Supplement Series 11 (Sheffield: JSOT Press, 1986).
2. Richard Bauckham, "The Economic Critique of Rome in Revelation 18," in *The Climax of Prophecy* (Edinburgh: T. & T. Clark, 1993), 338–83, esp. 350–71, dealing with the list of twenty-eight imports mentioned in 18:11–13.
3. M. Eugene Boring, *Revelation*, Interpretation 23 (Louisville, Ky.: John Knox Press, 1989), 161, 163.
4. For a recent discussion of the complicated issues, see Bauckham, "Nero and the Beast," in *The Climax of Prophecy*, 384–452.
5. Allan A. Boesak, *Comfort and Protest: Reflections on the Apocalypse of John of Patmos* (Philadelphia: Westminster Press, 1987).
6. Paul Boyer gives a long list of examples in *When Time Shall Be No*

More (Cambridge, Mass.: Harvard University Press, Belknap Press, 1992), 281–90.

7. The older but still valuable commentary by Isbon T. Beckwith, *The Apocalypse of John* (Grand Rapids: Baker Book House, reprinted 1967; original copyright by Macmillan Co., 1919), spends pp. 342–93 on the question of authorship, most of them (pp. 362–93) in very fine print.

8. For two examples of this reevaluation of Christian persecution under Domitian, see Adela Yarbro Collins, *Crisis and Catharsis* (Philadelphia: Westminster Press, 1984), 69–73, and the more detailed study by Leonard Thompson, *The Book of Revelation: Apocalypse and Empire* (New York: Oxford University Press, 1990), 95–115.

9. Collins, *Crisis and Catharsis*, 84–110.

Chapter 15. Persecution Ethics

1. Charles Homer Giblin, S. J., *The Book of Revelation*, Good News Studies 34 (Collegeville, Minn.: A Michael Glazier Book of the Liturgical Press, 1991), esp. 25–35, 222–31. He suggests that the holy war imagery determines the structure of Revelation 4—22, although this pushes beyond the text at some points. Also valuable is Richard Bauckham, *The Climax of Prophecy* (Edinburgh: T. & T. Clark, 1993), 210–37, and his *The Theology of the Book of Revelation* (Cambridge: Cambridge University Press, 1993), 66–108.

2. M. Eugene Boring gives four reasons behind John's advice, in *Revelation*, Interpretation 23 (Louisville, Ky.: John Knox Press, 1989), 188.

3. Adela Yarbro Collins, *Crisis and Catharsis* (Philadelphia: Westminster Press, 1984), 132–34, deals with the broad issues but not with the mark of the beast.

Chapter 16. John's Theological Vision

1. Carol Christ, "Feminist Liberation Theology and Yahweh as Holy Warrior: An Analysis of Symbol," in *Women's Spirit Bonding*, ed. Janet Kalven and Mary I. Buckley (New York: Pilgrim Press, 1984), 201–12; the quote is from 205.

2. Daphne Hampson, *Theology and Feminism*, Signposts in Theology (Oxford: Basil Blackwell, 1990), 151–55.

3. Tina J. Pippin, *Death and Desire* (Louisville, Ky.: Westminster/ John Knox Press, 1992).

4. Arthur P. Mendel, *Vision and Violence* (Ann Arbor, Mich.: University of Michigan Press, 1992).
5. This point is made effectively by Richard Nysee, "Yahweh Is a Warrior," in *Word and World* 7 (1987): 192–201.
6. Richard Bauckham, *The Theology of the Book of Revelation* (Cambridge: Cambridge University Press, 1993), 42–43.
7. M. Eugene Boring, *Revelation*, Interpretation 23 (Louisville, Ky.: John Knox Press, 1989), 112–19 (on "Interpreting Revelation's Violent Imagery"), and 176–78 (on Armageddon).
8. Cited in David Heller, *Reinventing Government* (Reading, Mass.: Addison-Wesley Publishing Co., 1992), xiii.
9. Walter Wink explores a strategy for nonviolent resistance, based on biblical insights, in *Engaging the Powers* (Minneapolis: Fortress Press, 1992).

BIBLIOGRAPHY

Books in this short bibliography deal only with Revelation, not with other topics we have covered. Commentaries deal only with English translations, not with the Greek text. Titles mentioned in the notes are not included.

GOOD PLACES TO BEGIN

Efird, James M. *Revelation for Today*. Nashville: Abingdon Press, 1989.

Eller, Vernard. *The Most Revealing Book of the Bible*. Grand Rapids: Wm. B. Eerdmans Publishing Co., 1974.

Metzger, Bruce M. *Breaking the Code*. Nashville: Abingdon Press, 1993.

Mounce, Robert H. *What Are We Waiting For?* Grand Rapids: Wm. B. Eerdmans Publishing Co., 1992.

Prévost, Jean-Pierre, *How to Read the Apocalypse*. Translated by John Bowden and Margaret Lydamore. New York: Crossroad, 1993.

Richard, Pablo. *Apocalypse: A People's Commentary on the Book of Revelation*. Maryknoll, N.Y.: Orbis Books, 1995. In the original Spanish, the subtitle is "the reconstruction of hope."

COMMENTARIES

Barclay, William. *The Revelation of John*. Revised edition, 2 vols. Philadelphia: Westminster Press, 1976.

Caird, G. B. *The Revelation of St. John the Divine*. New York: Harper & Row, 1966.

Collins, Adela Yarbro. *The Apocalypse*. New Testament Message, vol. 22. Wilmington, Del.: Michael Glazier, 1979.

Harrington, Wilfrid J., O.P. *Understanding the Apocalypse*. Washington, D.C.: Corpus Books, 1969.

——. *Revelation*. Sacra Pagina, vol. 16. Michael Glazier Book. Collegeville, Minn.: Liturgical Press, 1993.

Ladd, George Eldon. *The Revelation of John*. Grand Rapids: Wm. B. Eerdmans Publishing Co., 1972.

Roloff, Jurgen. *The Revelation of John*. Translated by John E. Alsup. Minneapolis: Fortress Press, 1993. More technical.

Wall, Robert W. *Revelation*. New International Biblical Commentary. Peabody, Mass.: Hendrickson Publishers, 1991.

GENERAL STUDIES

Ewing, Ward. *The Power of the Lamb*. Cambridge, Mass.: Cowley Publications, 1990.

Michaels, J. Ramsey. *Interpreting the Book of Revelation*. Guides to New Testament Exegesis 7. Grand Rapids: Baker Book House, 1992.

Minear, Paul S. *New Testament Apocalyptic*. Interpreting Biblical Texts. Nashville: Abingdon Press, 1981.

Schüssler, Elisabeth Fiorenza. *The Book of Revelation: Justice and Judgment*. Philadelphia: Fortress Press, 1985.

Wainwright, Arthur W. *Mysterious Apocalypse: Interpreting the Book of Revelation*. Nashville: Abingdon Press, 1993. A history of interpretation.

SCRIPTURE INDEX

OLD TESTAMENT